RED GUIDE

97 0706354935

The Dorset Coast

Lyme Regis Bridport
Weymouth Portland
Dorchester Corfe
Swanage etc

Edited by Reginald J. W. Hammond

Second Edition—*Reprint*

WARD, LOCK LIMITED
116 BAKER STREET, LONDON, W.1.

Maps and Plans

Lyme Regis (plan) . . . . . *Page 6*

Bridport, West Bay (plan) . . . . *Page 28*

Weymouth (plan) . . . . . *Pages 56-57*

Archaeology, Weymouth District . . . *Page 74*

Portland . . . . *Page 85*

Swanage (plan) . . . . . . *Page 112*

Archaeology and Antiquities, Swanage District . . *Page 122*

This Guide covers the coast of Dorset, and includes the principal resorts of Lyme Regis, Bridport, Weymouth and Swanage, together with the many places of interest that may be visited from those centres.

Printed in Great Britain by Northumberland Press Ltd., Gateshead on Tyne

Contents

	PAGE
Lyme Regis	7
Walks from Lyme Regis	18
The Landslip	18
Uplyme	19
Combpyne and Rousdon	19
Axminster	20
Lambert's Castle and Coney's Castle	22
Charmouth	23
Forde Abbey	26
Bridport	29
West Bay	35
Excursions from Bridport and West Bay	36
Eype and Chideock	36
Whitchurch Canonicorum and Lambert's Castle	38
Bradpole and Loders	39
Beaminster and Broadwindsor	40
Burton Bradstock	44
Weymouth	45
Walks from Weymouth	59
The Nothe, Sandsfoot Castle and Rodwell	59
Wyke Regis, The Fleet and Chesil Beach	61
Radipole, Nottington, Broadwey and Upwey	63
Chickerell, Langton Herring, Buckland Ripers	66
Preston, Sutton Poyntz, The White Horse, Osmington and Osmington Mills	67
Upwey, Bincombe, Chalbury	69
Broadmayne, Whitcombe, The Winterbornes	70
Excursions from Weymouth	71
Portland	85
Dorchester	93
Sherborne	106
Swanage	113

Short Excursions from Swanage 120
  Peveril Point 120
  Durlston Head, Tilly Whim Caves, Great Globe and Anvil
    Point 121
  Ballard Down and Old Harry Rocks 125
  Studland 126
  To Corfe 129
  The Purbeck Quarries 129
  St. Aldhelm's Head 132
  Kingston 134
  Chapman's Pool 134
  To Bournemouth, New Forest, Salisbury . . . 135
  Poole Harbour 136
Corfe 140
  Excursions from Corfe 144
Wool, Bindon Abbey 147
Lulworth Cove: Bovington and Moreton . . . 148
Wareham . . . . . : . . 152
Index 159

Illustrations

Faces page

Lyme Regis Seafront 32
Lyme Regis from the Cobb 32
West Bay 33
Weymouth and the Bay 33
Osmington Mills 48
Chesil Beach and Portland Harbour . . . 48
Portland Bill 49
Cerne Abbas 49
Swanage 128
Swanage Bay and Ballard Down . . . 128
The Great Globe 129
Tilly Whim Caves 129
Durlston Bay 144
Studland Bay 144
Lulworth Cove 145
Corfe and the Castle 145

THE RED GUIDES

With Maps, Plans and Illustrations

Aberystwyth
Anglesey and North Wales

Barmouth, etc.
Bournemouth and District
Broads
Bude and North Cornwall

Channel Islands
Cornwall: North
Cornwall: South
Cornwall: West
Cotswolds
Cromer, Sheringham

Devon: North-west
Devon: South
Devon: South-east
Dorset Coast

Eastbourne, Seaford, etc.
Exeter and S.E. Devon
Exmoor and Doone Country

Falmouth and S. Cornwall

Ilfracombe and N.W. Devon
Isle of Man
Isle of Wight

Kent Coast

Lake District
Llandudno, Colwyn Bay
London
Lyme Regis and District
Lynton and Lynmouth

New Forest
Newquay and N. Cornwall
Norfolk, North

Peak District
Penzance and W. Cornwall

St. Ives and W. Cornwall
Stratford upon Avon
Sussex Coast: East
Sussex Coast: West
Swanage, Corfe, etc.

Tenby and South Wales
Thames, inc. Oxford
Torquay and District

Wales, N. (Northn. Section)
Wales, N. (Southn. Section)
Wales, South
Weymouth and District
Wye Valley

Yorkshire Coast
Yorkshire Dales

SCOTLAND

Aberdeen, Deeside, etc.
Edinburgh and District
Glasgow and the Clyde
Highlands

Inverness, Strathpeffer, etc.
Northern Scotland
Oban, Fort William, etc.
Western Scotland

RED TOURIST GUIDES

Baddeley's Guide to the Lake District
The Complete Guide to Scotland

The Complete Guide to Ireland
The Complete Guide to Wales

WARD, LOCK & CO., LIMITED

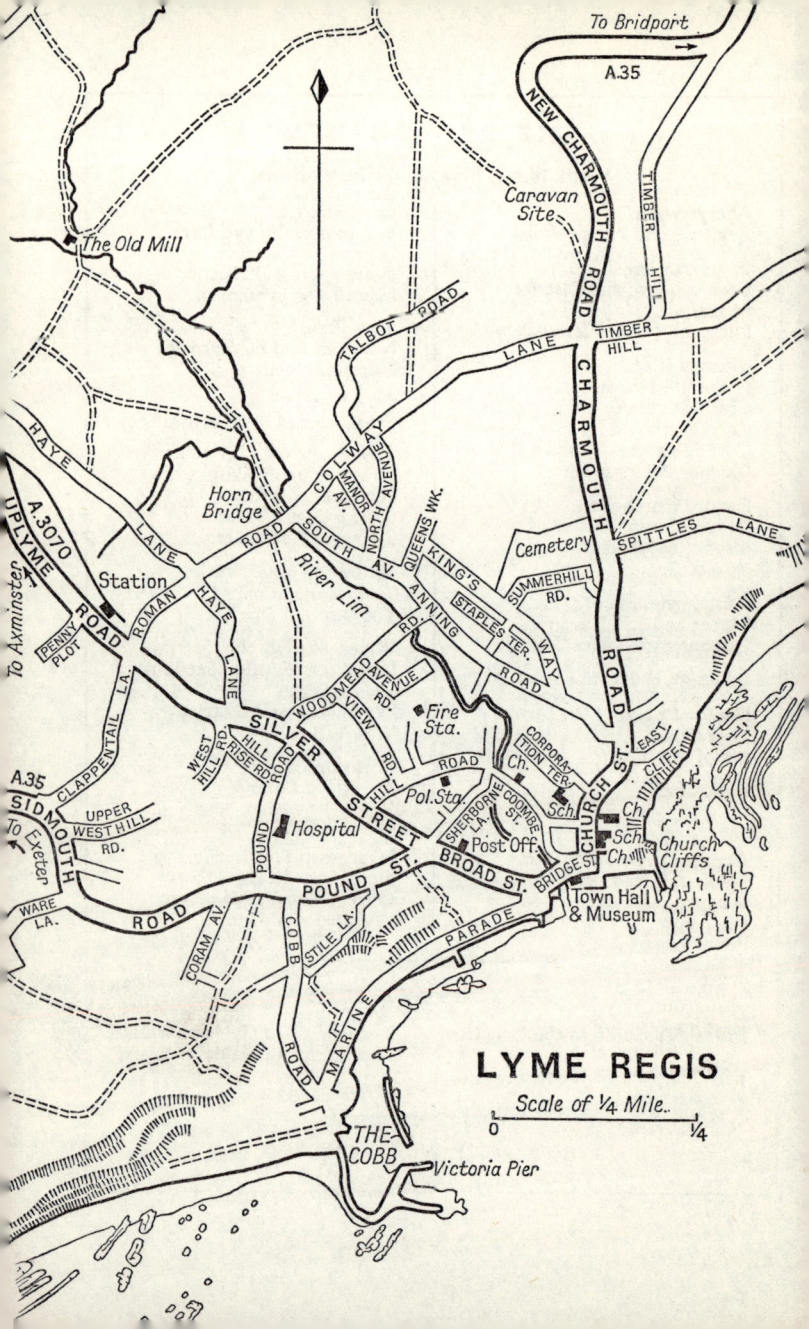

LYME REGIS

Scale of ¼ Mile..

Lyme Regis

General Information

Banks.—*Lloyds; Midland*—both in Broad Street.

Buses.—Devon General and Southern National run frequent buses to Exeter, Sidmouth, Seaton, Rousdon, Axminster, Bridport, Weymouth. There are daily tours and long-distance runs during the season.

Car Parks.—Cobb Gate, Monmouth Beach, The Square, Station Garage, Watson's, Broad Street, Cloverdale, Charmouth Road, Woodmead Hall, Hill Road, Holmbush.

Churches and Chapels. (For Service times, see local announcements)

St. Michael's (Parish Church), Church Street.

Peek Memorial Chapel, Pound Street.

Methodist, Church Street.

Baptist, Silver Street.

Roman Catholic (St. Michael and George), Silver Street.

Congregational, Coombe Street.

Plymouth Brethren, Gospel Hall, Coombe Street.

Council Offices.—Borough Offices, Broad Street. Information Bureau, Boat House, Marine Parade.

Distances.—Axminster, 6; Bridport, 10; Crewkerne, 17; Dorchester, 24; Exeter, 28; Exmouth, 27; Honiton, 15; London, 152; Seaton, 8; Sidmouth, 17; Taunton, 28; Weymouth, 29.

Early Closing.—Thursday.

Hotels.—*Royal Lion*, Broad Street, *Alexandra*, Pound Street; *Three Cups*, Broad Street; *Victoria*, Axminster Road; *Bay*, Seafront; *St. Michael's*, Pound Street; *Buena Vista*, Pound Street; *Stile House*, Pound Street; *Tudor House*, Church Street; *Shamien*, Pound Street; *High Cliff*, Sidmouth Road; *Coverdale Guest House*, Woodmead Road; and many others.

Licensing Hours.—10–2.30 and 6–10.30. Sundays 12–2 and 7–10.30.

Museum.—Bridge Street. Fossil collection.

Population.—About 3,500.

Post Office.—At top of Broad Street. 9–5.30.

Sport and Entertainment

Aquarium.—Marine aquarium, open daily in summer, Victoria Pier.

Bathing.—Good and safe. Beach is of shingle with sand at low tide. Bathing cabins, tents and deck chairs available.

Billiards and Snooker.—At the *Conservative Club*, fully licensed; visitors welcome.

Boating and Sailing.—Rowing and sailing boats for hire. Keen amateur sailing club welcomes visitors and holds races two or three times weekly. Clubroom is on Victoria Pier.

Bowls.—Excellent bowling green at the Cobb (Monmouth Beach). Woods and slips provided if required.

Cinema.—*Regent,* Broad Street.

Cricket.—Matches are played at Uplyme (opposite Talbot Arms Hotel). Visitors welcomed.

Dancing.—Dances are frequently held at the Woodmead Hall and at Marine Theatre.

Fishing.—Boatmen arrange fishing trips from the Cobb or Cobb Gate. Local fish are whiting, skate, plaice, mackerel and conger.

Golf.—Lyme Regis Golf Club is about a mile from the town; on Timber Hill on the Charmouth-Bridport bus route.

Putting Green.—At Langmoor Gardens.

Tennis.—Public hard courts in Hill Road. Open daily and bookable in advance.

Theatre.—*Marine Theatre,* Church Street. Variety, plays and various entertainments during the season.

Facing south and sheltered from northerly winds by a protecting background of hills, Lyme Regis is beautifully set in a steep combe opening on to a wide bay. The view seawards is magnificent, embracing miles of lovely coastline, including Golden Cap, Chesil Beach and Portland Bill.

Good bathing may be enjoyed from a shingle beach. At low tide the shingle is edged by a fine stretch of sand dotted with many pools, a delight to youngsters. There is boating in the bay, tennis courts in the valley and golf links high on a cliff overlooking the town. The streets slope sharply from the cliff top to the beach and promenade.

Broad Street, with post office, banks, shops and some of the larger hotels is the principal thoroughfare. From its lower end the **Marine Parade** stretches westward as a pedestrian way, there being no road for cars along this part of the front. At the far end of Marine Parade is—

The Cobb

an old stone pier forming an extensive harbour and believed to date from the time of Edward I. The origin of the name is unknown, but there are records of an ancient feast called the "Cobb Ale Feast". With a length of 870 feet the curve of the Cobb forms a fine promenade though its upper surface slopes to the sea at an appreciable angle. Its high wall makes it a double promenade and walkers have a choice of shelter or a glorious blow. The eastern section ends with the **Victoria Pier,** so-called after the Princess Victoria landed here with her mother in 1833. Picturesque buildings on the Cobb include headquarters of sailing and powerboat clubs while another houses a **Marine Aquarium** (*open daily*). Lyme was busy in former days both with local fishing and trading with distant ports.

Westward of the Cobb is the bowling green and the Western or **Monmouth's Beach.** The Duke landed about a hundred yards west of the wall. Here too a little later Judge Jeffreys caused twelve men to be executed for their part in the rebellion.

In view of the one-time importance of the harbour it is curious the actual town showed little disposition to spread this far westward and nothing but a track along the cliff edge provided direct communication. Wheeled traffic went round by the hilly Cobb Road and the even steeper Pound Street and Broad Street. Until recent times Lyme comprised a harbour section and a "church town", the latter being at the eastern end of the little bay.

The Parish Church

The Parish Church of St. Michael the Archangel is in Church Street at the foot of the town and about 100 feet from the sea. It was originally much farther inland, but the wet lias subsoil gradually slips seawards, making constant repairs and protective measures necessary. Owing to the steepness of the hillside, the floor of the church is at three different levels, the chancel being several feet higher than the porch and the floor of the nave sloping to the west.

The present church was built about 1500. There is evidence that earlier buildings existed on the site, and of the Norman one, the nave has survived and now forms the west porch, the two columns on the north side dating from about 1130. The lower part of the tower is thirteenth-century work, but the remainder has been considerably restored. Inside, the baptistery under the tower is modern.

The nave was completed about 1506. Note the graceful arches and the fine carving on the pillars showing initials or coats-of-arms. The old lectern now at the west end of the nave serves as a display case for a copy of Erasmus's *Paraphrase of St. Luke's Gospel* (1559), an old chained "Breeches" Bible and a copy of the "Bad" Bible of 1663. The large ancient tapestry on the north wall represents a Royal marriage—thought possibly the marriage of Henry VIII to Catherine in 1509.

The gallery is interesting for the inscription in the centre which reads: "John Hassard built this to the glorie of Almightie God in the eighteenth yeare of his age, ano domini 1611."

The finely carved Jacobean pulpit has an inscription round the canopy which reads: "To God's glory, Richard Harvey of London, Mercer and Merchant Adventurer 1613. Faith is by hearing." Harvey was three times elected as mayor.

A short distance above the church are the **Tudbold Almshouses,** bequeathed to the town by Thomas Tudbold, in 1548, but completely rebuilt in 1887. The tenements number four, but are not endowed. A later charitable bequest was that of Nicholas Marder, a master mariner, who, in 1892, left a sum of money for the building of six almshouses for old sailors. These houses are in Coombe Street.

At the foot of Church Street is a small " Market Place ", the Town Hall, and the Old Market.

The **Town Hall** was rebuilt on the site of the old Guildhall in 1887–8. It is used for the monthly meetings of the Borough Council. The assembly is referred to as the " Court of Hustings ", robes are worn and old traditions of procedure observed. The iron-cased door, that once led to the " lock-up ", is in the wall of the north front; many valuable records, documents and charters are preserved in the muniment room. Beneath the Town Hall is the **Old Market,** having in the upper storey a carved projecting window. At the side of the Market is an opening leading to the **Gun Cliff,** a small promenade with outlook towards Golden Cap and the grandly undulating cliffs on to Portland, and in the other direction across to the Cobb.

The **Museum** (*open* 10–1, 2.30–5.30) contains many items of local interest. Here are the old stocks, the Shambles Bell (1647), a man trap, and relics of Monmouth's Rebellion and the Siege of Lyme— cannon balls of various sizes, the rusty head of a boarding pike on which rebels' heads were exposed. Not least interesting are the series of documents from the Borough Records, displayed in frames and furnished with pithy " headlines ". Relics of the Assembly Rooms are shown, and there are also the oaken tracery of a window and the masonry of an aumbry from the Bridge Chapel, which was discovered when the cellers and foundations of adjoining cottages were excavated; and the hinges of the Cobb Gate. The geological specimens and fossils are extensive, and the museum includes a small geological library with a collection of topographical and historical books dealing with Lyme and Dorset generally.

Westward of the Town Hall, Bridge Street crosses the **Buddle Bridge.** For the antiquary no part of Lyme has such attractions as the old arch, thought to be of fourteenth- or fifteenth-century work, though there is nothing to indicate this age from the parapet. Originally the Bridge comprised two arches, the eastern one being buried in the foundations of the building adjoining the present bridge. The ancient pointed arch of dog-tooth-shaped stones closely cemented together is supposed to have been built in the twelfth century. It was discovered during the excavations which also revealed what is supposed to have been the **Bridge Chapel** or a priest's cell probably dating from the thirteenth to fourteenth centuries, relics from which may be seen in the museum. The only fragment of masonry of contemporary date with the buried arch is the Norman arch in the church.

In the neighbourhood of the Bridge are some of the older parts of Lyme, though modern improvements are altering these or sweeping them away altogether. **Coombe Street** is a narrow thoroughfare with here and there a few steps leading down beneath its buildings to the stream, and off it are on one side the old mill, and on the other George's Square and Monmouth Street. Turning down past the mill the path along the **Lynch** can be followed, opposite being gardens and enclosures sloping up to Broad Street. Coombe Street is rejoined where the steep Sherborne Lane turns off to the left, or one can continue along Mill Green beside the stream. This is said to be the old road out of the town. Sherborne Lane leads to the road junction at the top of **Broad Street.** Here **Silver Street** leads to Uplyme and Axminster and **Pound Street** to Seaton and Sidmouth. In Silver Street is the public library (*daily except Thursdays*). In Pound Street is—

The Peek Memorial Chapel

of interest as having been originally a stable. In 1844 the building was transformed into the private chapel of Poulett House (now the *Hotel Alexandra*) by its owner, the Rev. Edward Peek, and in 1901 it was given to the parish by the Hon. Lady Peek. It is a small gabled building with a bell turret. Inside is a continuous and coloured wagon-head ceiling. The altar-piece is a Venetian mosaic depicting " Our Lord in Majesty".

Adjoining the chapel is the main entrance to the **Langmoor Gardens**—a pleasantly laid out stretch of turf with flower beds, tree-shaded seats and a putting green. A path gives direct access through the gardens to the Parade and offers a pleasanter route than that *via* Broad Street or the steep Cobb Road.

FROM THE HISTORY OF LYME

Lyme Regis ranks as one of the oldest "loyal and ancient Boroughs" in Britain. The earliest authentic reference to the town is the grant by Cynewulf, or Kenwulf, king of West Saxony (755–784), who by charter dated 774 assigned to the religious fraternity at Sherborne Abbey "the land of one mansion near the west bank of the river Lim, and not far from the place where it falls into the sea, so that salt for the said church should be boiled there for the supplying of various wants". From 705 to 1075 Lyme formed part of the diocese of Sherborne (the name of Sherborne Lane, at the top of Broad Street, perpetuates the ancient connection). Since then it has been attached to Salisbury. Edward I enfranchised Lyme, granting it the liberties of a haven and a borough. It is supposed that the Cobb was built during this reign as a protection to the town's small fishing fleet, and for the convenience of the vessels that ventured to trade with the Continent. In consequence of the reversion of Sherborne Abbey and the manor to the Crown in the time of Edward I, the dependencies of the Abbey likewise changed ownership, and Lyme henceforth assumed the appellation "Regis".

The Ancient Port. In Edward III's reign the port was in a prosperous condition, with a fair amount of over-sea commerce. In 1347 came the royal levy for ships to besiege Calais. Lyme responded with four vessels fitted for war (Portsmouth sent only five), and sixty-two men. Retaliation came later, when the French landed on several occasions (*temp*. Henry IV and V) and fired and sacked the town.

13

In 1377 the Cobb, on the welfare of which the well-being of the town depended, sustained serious damage from storms, and the town itself suffered injury. Successive petitions for assistance to repair the Cobb met with little success, and under the Tudors the town suffered much by the inroads of the sea. The first stanza of Michael Drayton's *Battle of Agincourt* is interesting to Dorset folk, as showing the contribution Dorset made to the fleet which took the English army to France in 1415.

> " So Lyme three ships into the Navy sent,
> Of which the *Sampson* scarce a month before
> Had sprung a plank, and her main-mast had spent,
> With extreme peril that she got to shore.
> With them five other out of Weymouth went,
> Which by Southampton were made up a score,
> With those that rode at pleasure in the bay,
> And that at anchor before Portsmouth lay."

In 1535 Lyme received help from the Crown, in the shape of an annual grant of £20, charged upon the Customs receipts of Poole, which subsidy was still being paid in 1619. In spite of this annuity, Nicholas Wadham reported to the Government that the men of Lyme had petitioned him concerning the bad state of the Cobb, saying they had been forced to pawn the cross and other jewels in their church, in the hope of obtaining King Henry's favour.

The chief local industries were the manufacture of serge and salt, and a fair Continental trade was maintained.

Lyme was well to the front during Armada days, and sent its quota of little ships to fight the Spaniards. The names of the vessels were *The Jacob* and *The Revenge*. The great fight began off Lyme Regis, and the townspeople from the heights saw it, and perhaps could follow the fortunes of their own tough little contingent. The news of Sir Richard Grenville's triumphant defeat in the *Revenge* (the one 'gainst the fifty-three) was brought by a Lyme ship.

In passing we may note that Bess Throckmorton, the cause of so much of Queen Elizabeth's fury against Raleigh, was the daughter of a Mayor of Lyme.

Queen Bess granted another charter to the town on condition " that the Mayor and Burgesses do keep up the Cobb ".

The Siege of Lyme during the Civil War was of more than local importance. Sir Walter Erle and Sir Thomas Trenchard took possession of the town in the name of the Parliament, and fortified it. The royal forces in the West were commanded by Sir Ralph Hopton and Lord Poulett of Hinton St. George, Somerset. In January, 1643, Ashe, the residence of the famous Drake family, near Axminster, fell into the hands of the Royalists, as did Stedcombe House, Axmouth, the residence of Sir Walter Erle. It is astonishing that Lyme, with its apparently untenable position, should have seriously opposed the powerful armies of Sir Ralph Hopton, Poulett, and Prince Maurice, whose estimate of the task before them was that it was "breakfast work". They even rashly declared they would not dine until the town had fallen—a boast they made haste to forget.

Enthusiasm stirred every man and woman in Lyme.

The garrison mustered 600 men. The women, it is recorded, even put on breeches to deceive the enemy, and fed the fighting line with ammunition. Protestantism was a strong factor, and gave great impetus to the struggle.

On April 20, 1644, when only Lyme and Poole were left for the King in the West, Prince Maurice, with an army of nearly 5,000 men, advanced to Uplyme and laid siege to the port—not because the place was of the slightest strategical importance, but because of the dreaded personal influence of the resolute defenders. Again and again the besiegers attacked, only to be repulsed, and the town in turn made sorties. Food was brought by sea, together with repeated thanks from Parliament for the brave defence.

For nearly two months the fighting continued without intermission, the lion's share falling to Captain Davey, who commanded one of the improvised forts. He worked his guns with amazing persistence, while his men never seemed to sleep. Other forts in the town's defences had to be abandoned, but the Royalists were powerless to silence Davey's fort. The storming parties lost as many as 400 men in one day. On June 15, Prince Maurice's army retired in disgrace, having lost 2,000 men in these desperate attacks. The defenders' loss amounted to 120.

Cannon balls of 17½ lb. weight have often been found on the sea-ledges, or dug up on the outskirts of the town; some are in the museum.

After the siege of Lyme Parliament made the defenders a grant of £2,000 and a supply of boots and shoes, as some recompense for the hardships they had suffered. One of the defenders of the town was Robert Blake (afterwards the famous admiral), who, as a reward for his services, was promoted to the rank of colonel.

The Landing of Monmouth. On June 11, 1685, James, Duke of Monmouth, a natural son of Charles II, landed at Lyme, on the beach at the back of the Cobb, and within a few days some 5,000 recruits had flocked to his standard, among them Daniel Defoe. The appearance of Monmouth's three ships, of foreign build and with no colours flying, caused much uneasiness in the town, and Macaulay tells us that "the uneasiness increased when it was found that the Custom-house officers, who had gone on board according to usage, did not return. The townspeople repaired to the cliffs, and gazed long and anxiously, but could find no solution of the mystery. At length seven boats put off from the largest of the strange vessels, and rowed to the shore. From these boats landed about eighty men, well armed and appointed. Among them were Monmouth, Gray, Fletcher, Ferguson, Wade, and Anthony Buyse, an officer who had been in the service of the Elector of Brandenburg.

"Monmouth knelt down and thanked God for having preserved the friends of liberty and pure religion from the perils of the sea, and implored the divine blessing on what was yet to be done by land. . . . As soon as it was known under what leader and for what purpose this expedition came, the enthusiasm of the populace burst through all restraints. The little town was in an uproar with men running to and fro, and shouting, 'A Monmouth! A Monmouth! The Protestant Religion!' Meanwhile the ensign of the adventurers, a blue flag, was set up in the market-place. The military stores were deposited in the town hall; and a declaration setting forth the objects of the expedition was read from the Cross."

After the defeat at Sedgemoor twelve local participants in the Rebellion were hanged on the exact spot on which Monmouth had landed. Judge Jeffreys refused all pleas for clemency even for the young and handsome lads William Hewling and Christopher Battiscombe, whose bodies lie in the churchyard at Lyme. As a warning against future uprisings, the mayor, a gentleman named Jones, notorious for his cruelty, having procured two of the heads of the rebels, placed them on pedestals in his garden at the Tower House in Broad Street, where they remained for many years.

In the Museum can be seen a piece of the wood which formed part of the gallows on which the rebels were hanged.

A Monmouth "Find". On April 24, 1786, a labourer named Kelway discovered among the ruins of a house at Lyme three small chests, filled with gold and silver coins to the amount of £2,000, chiefly of the period of Charles I and II, which are thought to have been buried for safety at the time of Monmouth's landing. Kelway informed his landlord of the find, and, the secret being discovered, all the neighbours rushed to the spot, and it is said there was scarcely a person present who did not come away the richer by sixty or seventy pounds.

Privateers. The ports of Lyme, Poole and Weymouth were the homes of many adventurous persons, who risked both life and money in fitting up privateers, or "private men of war", when the Royal Navy was not strong enough adequately to destroy the enemy's commerce. At Lyme the *Bonaventure* was rigged up as a privateer by William Kirkridge, chief magistrate of the borough in 1621. This ship was licensed to "lay aboard four mynyons and five falckons as armament". Some years later, Richard Alford, another ex-mayor, made a large fortune with the *Swan* and other privateers, until Cromwell withdrew all these commissions, on the ground that the Navy was very short of sailors.

Seventeenth-century Lyme. In 1688 William, Prince of Orange, landed some of his troops on the Cobb, he himself having proceeded to Torbay, where he landed at Brixham. "The Protestant Religion and a Free Parliament" gained the day, and James II fled the country.

During the next fifty years Lyme gradually decayed, the population grew less and less, and house after house became untenanted and ruinous. The war with France, after the Revolution, completely ruined the foreign trade, and even the purely local industries, such as lace-making and weaving, dwindled, until they ceased altogether.

The Revival of Lyme. Gradually, however, the wonderful air began to be recommended by doctors, and the safety of the beach for bathing, afforded by the Cobb, brought the place into repute when sea-bathing became fashionable. As a holiday resort Lyme enjoyed a flourishing and fashionable existence a hundred years before Bournemouth existed. By 1750, this quiet retreat was a rival to Bath, and by 1800, the one occupation of the inhabitants was to provide accommodation for the large and regular influx of visitors throughout the summer. The Assembly Rooms had a clientèle drawn from the highest social levels; and card parties and dances were held every evening. There is no doubt also that the geological finds of Mary Anning drew a considerable number of visitors to the spot.

In view of the modern popularity of the town and the arrangements made for the comfort and amusement of visitors, it is curious to recall that, as Mr. Wanklyn records in *Lyme Regis: a Retrospect:*

" Henry VIII issued an order that not more than 20 strangers were to land at Lyme Regis at one time, and in 1687 two men were presented to the Court Leet Jury for coming with their families to live at Lyme! " Again: " Certain strolling players on four different occasions, between 1621-3, came to Lyme Regis. Not only were they refused admission to the town; they were even paid to go away! "

The Courts Leet. The town has succeeded in retaining the greater number of its curious medieval customs, including the Courts Leet, while for more than seven hundred years the weekly Court of Hustings has been held. Edward I conferred on the burgesses of Lyme privileges similar to those enjoyed by the citizens of London, and although these relics of feudal legislation have their inconvenient side, students of history cannot fail to rejoice in the survival of the Courts Leet, which appoint all the members of the Corporation, excepting only the Town Clerk.

Excursions from Lyme

THE LANDSLIP

The most popular walk along the coast is westward through the famous Landslip which extends practically all the way from Lyme Regis to Seaton—a walking distance of 8 miles. Good walkers should allow hardly less than four hours for the tramp from Lyme to Seaton; but this leaves little time for sightseeing or halts by the way. A whole day is not too long if the excursion is to be made in comfort. *Walkers are warned of the friable nature of the cliffs and that dense undergrowth frequently covers parts of the path.*

From Lyme Regis the best way to the Landslip is by the path leading from the car park by **Coram Tower,** at the junction of Cobb Road and Pound Street. Beyond Ware Cliffs and Pinhay Bay a path along the cliff leads to Seaton *via* the golf course.

There is a frequent bus service between Seaton and Lyme, or the return walk can be made *via* Axmouth and Rousdon to Sidmouth Road leading to Lyme.

A feature that always attracts the attention of those passing up or down Sidmouth Road is the old house known, from the shape of its roof, as the *Umbrella Cottage*. It is a small thatched cottage with a conical roof. It has traceried windows and a carved doorway, while carved owls appear on the capitals of the two front pillars.

The Great Landslip, so called to distinguish it from many slips of smaller extent, took place on Christmas Day, 1839. During the whole of Christmas Day the subsidence continued, and by the night of the 27th the land had settled down into very much the position we see it today, with a chasm about three-quarters of a mile long, by 400 feet wide, and varying from 100 to 150 feet in depth. Parallel with the coast a reef was forced up about a mile in length and 40 feet in height, covered with marine plants and shellfish of all descriptions, but shortly afterwards this reef subsided and disappeared from view.

In February, 1840, another landslip occurred at Whitlands, but on a much smaller scale, and on October 3, 1911, a subsidence took place on the Rousdon estate. More recently still other slips have occurred, and from the appearance of the cliffs it is obvious that others are imminent. Almost the whole distance between Lyme and the Axe is fallen cliff.

The land all around Lyme, and inland towards Axminster, is broken and rugged. What Nature has done elsewhere on a gigantic scale she has done here in miniature. Nothing could be more curious or fantastic than the shapes given to these acres of broken land. Here, on a small scale, are hills and ravines, mountain ranges and valleys, crags and precipices, pinnacles and chasms, all covered with creeper-hung trees and bracken.

TO UPLYME

Less than two miles north-west of Lyme Regis is Uplyme, just over the Devon border. It can be reached *via* Coombe Street and the path beside the Lym, turning left at Horn Bridge up Haye Lane or continuing along the Lym past the old mills towards Rhode Hill and Harcombe.

From the *Talbot Arms* return by way of Gore Lane.

An attractive route is *via* Ware Cross and the railway viaduct. Turn right at the *Talbot Arms* for the road back to Lyme. (Both routes about 4 miles.)

A longer excursion of about 12 miles is *via* Combpyne up to Trinity Hill, Hartgrove and the Beacon to Hunter's Lodge to Yawl, or, a shorter route from Hartgrove down Woodhouse Hill direct to Uplyme.

Uplyme is in Devon. Its parish church was much restored in the middle of last century and has Early English and Perpendicular features. A yew tree in the churchyard is notable. In 774 the area now called Uplyme belonged to the Abbot of Glastonbury. The steward's residence was probably where the *Devon Hotel* now stands. In the old cellars or cidery of this hotel is an oak beam reputed to be 1,500 years old, and a thirteenth-century skew passage. Also of interest is the dining-room with some fine panelling and a magnificent armorial fireplace.

TO COMBPYNE AND ROUSDON

Combpyne is about 3 miles west of Lyme Regis. The Coly-ford and Seaton buses pass near to it. Motorists and those not pressed for time may visit it in the course of a pleasant little

10-mile run as follows: From Lyme follow Silver Street past the station and through Uplyme to *Hunter's Lodge Inn*, where turn left. In a few hundred yards turn left into a narrower road which soon opens out on to heathland, with wonderful views to the westward. At its highest point, **Trinity Hill,** this road is nearly 700 feet above the sea. Skirt the Common for just over 3 miles, and immediately after crossing railway turn to the right and so down to Combpyne.

For walkers, a pleasant route is *via* Uplyme and the viaduct as on p. 19. Pass under the viaduct to a gate on the right opening on to a lane which passes through a farm and then leads upwards to Combpyne. To return to Lyme, turn left at the old Combpyne station to gain the Lyme–Seaton road (bus route) which in two miles leads to Lyme Regis.

Combpyne has an interesting thirteenth-century church, with an Early English lancet window, a piscina, a leper squint and an unusual tower arch. The chalice and paten are pre-Reformation plate, and have been in use for over four hundred and fifty years. The Communion cup is one of the rare type having toes on the feet. The tenor bell, one of the oldest in Devon, has a curious clapper and inscription.

From the south end of the village a road leads to **Rousdon.** The handsome modern building in the village is Rousdon House, built in 1878 by a former member of the Peek family. It is now occupied by Allhallows School removed here from Honiton in 1938.

TO AXMINSTER

Route.—*By road:* Leave Lyme Regis by Silver Street on A3070. at Hunter's Lodge turn left along A373 for Axminster. Frequent bus service.

Hotels.—*George; Old Bell; Cedar; Lamb Inn; Old White Hart; Red Lion.*

Axminster is a quiet but bright little town of some 3,000 people. It is best worth seeing on a Thursday when a lively market is held in the square with near-by market for the cattle trade. Pleasantly situated in the valley of the Axe in Devonshire, yet close to the borders of Somerset and Dorset, Axminster is a good holiday centre. There are comfortable hotels, hunting and excellent facilities for fishing trout, salmon and sea-trout (permits from *Old Bell Hotel*). The *George Hotel* is an attractive coaching inn with an Adam assembly room and musicians' gallery.

The **Church,** in the centre of the town, is an interesting building in various styles. Here in 786 was interred the body of Cynehard the Atheling, but few traces of the Saxon church have remained. The thirteenth-century tower probably rests on a pre-Norman substructure. There is a Norman doorway outside the east end of the south aisle and parts of the chancel (which is deflected) are of Early Decorated work, while the remainder of the church is Perpendicular. Note the squints through the eastern piers of the tower and also the handsome eighteenth-century candelabra under the tower. The Jacobean carving on the reading-desk and the pulpit date from 1663. The tolling bell, cast in 1647, used to be rung to celebrate the completion of a carpet.

Axminster achieved renown through the efforts of Thomas Whitty, the inventor and first manufacturer of the famous—

Axminster Carpets.—About the year 1754, Whitty saw in a London warehouse some fine specimens of Turkey carpets, woven without seams. After many experiments, extending over twelve months, Whitty succeeded in making on his looms a small piece of carpet resembling the Turkish model; and a little later he began to make a complete carpet, his children and relatives assisting. The carpet, being finished, excited great curiosity, and several orders were given to the manufacturer. Due to the help and encouragement of Lord and Lady Shaftesbury the industry grew and flourished; orders poured in from all parts of the country in such quantities that the looms could hardly keep pace with the demand. Increasing competition, and the need for economical working, coupled with a decrease of orders, however, led to the transfer of the looms to Wilton in 1835. In 1937 a new carpet factory was established in the town and the manufacture of Axminster carpets is again a thriving industry. A piece of an original carpet can be seen at the Council Chambers, Oak House.

About 2 miles south of Axminster, on the Seaton road, is **Ashe House,** at one time the home of the Drake family. Here, in 1650, was born John Churchill, afterwards the great Duke of Marlborough. His mother was Elizabeth Drake, who married Winston Churchill; but the Tavistock family, to which the famous Sir Francis Drake belonged, were connected but remotely with these Drakes. It is now a Poultry Breed Preservation Centre and many varieties of domestic fowl may be seen (*open certain afternoons*).

A long mile south of Ashe is the village of **Musbury,** beneath the down crowned with a hill castle, of the same name. The church contains a striking Drake monument, large figures of three members with their wives kneeling before *Prie-Dieu*.

TO LAMBERT'S CASTLE AND CONEY'S CASTLE

Road Route.—Leave Lyme by way of Silver Street and A3070 to **Hunter's Lodge.** Here follow B3165 to Marshwood and Birdsmoor Gate. The return can be varied by taking B3162 to Chard and regain Lyme Regis *via* Axminster.
Walkers should take the foregoing route on the outward journey (bus to *Hunter's Lodge Inn*). Return same way or via Coney's Castle (see below).

Northward from Lyme is a ridge of high ground separating the valleys of the *Axe* and *Char*. From *Hunter's Lodge Inn* to Lambert's Castle the crest of the ridge is marked by a good road running between 600 and 800 feet above sea-level. Trees screen most of the views on either hand, but **Lambert's Castle** is a great bare turfy eminence from which a wonderful panorama of the whole horizon can be enjoyed. The Castle, 842 feet above sea-level, was an important British earthwork having triple mounds and ditches, pierced by three entrances. The camp is D-shaped, and covers an area of 12 acres. It received its name from Canute who, on being baptized, took the Christian name of Lambert. The area is now held by the National Trust and is an ideal spot for picnics. A track leaves the road so that cars may be drawn up on the down.

Good walkers desiring an alternative return route should follow the south-easterly ridge from Lambert's Castle to **Coney's Castle,** a subsidiary encampment less than a mile distant (*see* p. 25). From the Castle continue to follow the ridge-line, with a good view in front of **Conygar Hill.**

Charmouth

Access.—Bus services from Lyme Regis (3 miles), Axminster (6 miles), Bridport (6 miles).

By Road. Charmouth is situated on the old London-Exeter main road, 145 miles from London. There are regular coach services from principal centres.

Angling.—Trout fishing in the *Char.* Bass and mackerel in the bay.

Bank.—*Lloyds.*

Bathing.—The beach is mainly shingle with stretches of coarse sand at low tide. Safe bathing. Chalets.

Churches and Chapels.—*St. Andrew's Parish Church,* High Street; *Congregational,* High Street; *Roman Catholic* at Lyme Regis and Chideock.

Dancing.—At various halls in the village.

Early Closing.—Wednesday or Thursday.

Golf.—At Timber Hill, *see* p. 8.

Hotels.—*Coach and Horses; Queen's Arms; Sea Horse; Hammond's Mead; Charmouth House; New Inn; George; Royal Oak.*

Population.—900.

Pott Office.—In main street.

Sport.—Tennis, Bowls and Putting. Cricket and Football. Playing field. *Charmouth Lawn Tennis Club* in Sea Lane. Tournament in August.

Charmouth lies astride the main road about half a mile from the sea, and has greatly developed in recent years. The little town faces south and being sheltered by steep hills on the north, is warm. The surrounding scenery is splendid and from the summit of the coastal hills all view-points afford a superb panorama. On the east side is a peak crowned with a triangular patch of yellow sandstone which glowing with reflected sunlight

23

is appropriately known as **Golden Cap** (619 feet), *see* p. 25.

Charmouth has a long history; it figures in Saxon records and is mentioned in Domesday Book as the Manor of Cernemude. Today, the village consists mainly of one steep street, flanked by buildings of different periods and varying styles—thatched cottages, ancient inns, Georgian houses and modern residences. The river Char is spanned by two stone bridges; the one at the eastern end of the street bears an old metal plaque, threatening transportation for life to any person who damages the bridge. Near by is a toll house, a relic of the days of private turnpike roads.

Halfway up the street is the **Parish Church,** dedicated to St. Andrew. This was rebuilt and enlarged in 1836, on the site of a medieval one, which in its turn, had been "Reedifyed and Beautified by Anth Ellesdon, Esq 1732", as we learn from the inscription on the stone over the west door. Little remains of the former church, except the north porch and a few fragments of stone, but there is a model of it near the vestry. The fine east window was designed by Christopher Webb.

The *Queen's Armes Hotel* is an interesting old building in which Charles II spent a night on his unsuccessful attempt to leave the country by way of Charmouth. It has a new front but the interior retains old features, including a Gothic window, stone fireplaces, a carved ceiling and panelled wall. A large chimney is said to have served as a hiding-place, and the room in which Charles is said to have slept may still be seen. Catherine of Aragon stayed here in 1501 and her badge can be seen worked in the plaster of a bedroom. The house appears to have been a guest house of Forde Abbey. A doorway built by Thomas Chard, the last abbot, has been uncovered, while the monks' oven was discovered in the side of the large chimney.

The house carries a commemorative tablet similar to that placed on Ellesdon Farm, the *George Inn,* Bridport, and on the *George Inn*, Broadwindsor, at each of which Charles II stayed.

Another interesting Charmouth hostelry is the *George Hotel*, a seventeenth-century coaching inn with a quaint projecting window over the porch. The *George Hotel* was a stopping place for the Bridport–Lyme coach. Passengers waited in the little room over the porch from which they could see its approach.

From the main street, roads lead to the beach. Those on foot can go via **Higher Sea Lane,** but cars must take **Lower Sea Lane,** where are the Church Hall, the Council Offices and the Charmouth Lawn Tennis Club, and car parks. On the opposite side of the main street, a road leads to the attractive playing fields where there are a putting course, tennis courts and a well-tended bowling green, in addition to cricket and football pitches and a playground reserved and equipped for children.

Fossils abound in the adjacent cliffs, where the various strata are also finely shown. It was at **Black Ven,** nearly midway between Charmouth and Lyme, that Mary Anning discovered the celebrated specimen of the Ichthyosaurus. In addition to its geological fame, Black Ven commands one of the finest views in Dorset.

Charmouth is a place of some antiquity, and a short distance northward are two very ancient earthworks, **Coney's Castle** and Lambert's Castle, the former said to have been the camp of Egbert when he fought the Danes. The Saxon Chronicle thus records the battle: " A.D. 833, King Egbert fought against the men of the thirty-five ships at Charmouth, and there was great slaughter made, and the Danish men maintained possession of the field."

The footpath route from Charmouth begins almost opposite the end of the lane from the beach. For a mile and a half it winds between the hills, meeting the lanes in the vicinity of Wootton Fitzpaine. Here a choice of routes is offered: a path climbing the western flank of the tongue of high ground crowned by the Castle, and a lane from Wootton Cross taking a more easterly line.

For **Lambert's Castle,** a mile north of Coney's Castle, *see* p. 22.

Charmouth to Golden Cap. A popular walk generally beginning at Charmouth, Morecombelake or Chideock, is to the high cliff crowned with a stratum of sandy gravel which (viewed from the seaward side) has earned it the name of **Golden Cap.**

One route—a longish walk—begins just over the second bridge at Charmouth by the lane ascending Stonebarrow Hill; another is from the beach at Charmouth near the car park, climbing the cliff and following the coast (but keep well away from the crumbling cliff edge). The shortest route begins by the path beside the little chapel about ¼ mile beyond the *Ship Inn*, Morecombelake. The path goes down across the fields, to a farmyard, through which it passes into the fields again. Beyond the second field is a lane. Turn left for some three hundred yards, go through gate on right and cross field to a cottage, from which the path continues across fields to Golden Cap.

A return can be made *via* **Seatown,** a cluster of houses at the foot of

25

the eastern flank of Golden Cap, where teas, etc., may be obtained and whence it is but a mile to Chideock (*see* p. 36). Good walkers will enjoy the rather arduous walk along the cliffs beyond Seatown to Eype Mouth by way of Thorncombe Beacon (509 feet) and so to West Bay.

FORDE ABBEY

Admission.—The house and gardens are open to the public, 2-6 p.m., on Wednesdays, May to September inclusive, and on certain Sundays, including those of the Spring, Summer and Autumn Bank Holiday week-ends. But see local announcements. Charge.

The old Abbey, now a private residence, was formerly in Devon, but was transferred to Dorset in 1842, together with the parish of Thorncombe, in which it is situated. The author of the *Book of the Axe* described the Abbey as "one of the most perfect of the numerous remains of those magnificent conventual establishments with which the country was anciently studded".

The history of the monastery began in the early twelfth century when Sir Richard Brioniis founded an abbey at Brightley in Devon with twelve Cistercian monks from Waverley Abbey in Surrey. The story is to the effect that after five years at Brightley the monks decided to leave in consequence of the barrenness of the soil, and

26

they set out for Waverley. On their journey they passed through Thorncombe, where Sir Richard's sister Adelicia gave them a site for a new abbey, which, owing to its proximity to a ford over the River Axe, became known as Forde Abbey.

The choice of the site was influenced by the position of the river, an almost invariable accompaniment to a Cistercian monastery. On the high ground at Forde, a small spring formed a stream which flowed northwards into the river, and this stream was used in the industrial court, where it worked the corn mill, the saw-mill, and the other mechanical appliances.

The Abbey was well endowed, and many old Devonshire families, including the de Pomeroys and the Courtenays, enriched the monastic coffers from time to time.

The Abbey church, of which nothing remains, was built on the south side of the monastery, on the north ran the river, a necessary drainage. With the exception of the church and the infirmary the original monastic buildings remain intact, and include the Chapter House (now a private chapel), dormitory, undercroft, or novitiate school, a twelfth-century refectory, a meat-eater's refectory built above it, kitchen, and one side of the cloister. The buildings were much restored by Thomas Chard, the last abbot of Forde in 1521. It was he who built the Great Hall, the Tower, and rebuilt the Cloister in the Perpendicular style before work was brought to a halt by the Dissolution in 1538. The property subsequently changed hands several times and was eventually purchased by Sir Edmund Prideaux, Attorney-General to Cromwell, in 1649. He converted the building for residential use, altering the central staircase, the saloon and outside portico and built rooms over the cloister.

The Mortlake Tapestries. A staircase leads to the Saloon, 58 feet long and 25 feet in height. There hang the tapestries which, more than anything else, drew art lovers to Forde Abbey from all parts of the world. The tapestries are from cartoons by Raphael, and now in the Victoria and Albert Museum. They were made at Mortlake by Brussels weavers, brought over by Charles I to instruct English workers in such tapestry work. They were later given by Queen Anne to Sir Francis Gwyn, the then owner of Forde Abbey and Her Majesty's Secretary for War. The cartoons from which they were worked were drawn for Pope Leo X by Raphael, and more than one set of tapestries is known to have been worked from the designs. Those at Forde, however, are very fine and have borders thought to have been designed by Rubens.

The scenes represented are:—
1. The scene at Lystra described in Acts xiv.
2. The Saviour's charge to St. Peter.
3. SS. Peter and John healing the lame man at the gate of the Temple.
4. Ananias and Sapphira.
5. The miraculous draught of fishes.

The **Gardens** surrounding the Abbey are of great beauty, and extend over fifteen acres. There are a great many fine trees, shady ponds and water gardens, flowering shrubs of great variety, herbaceous borders and rock gardens.

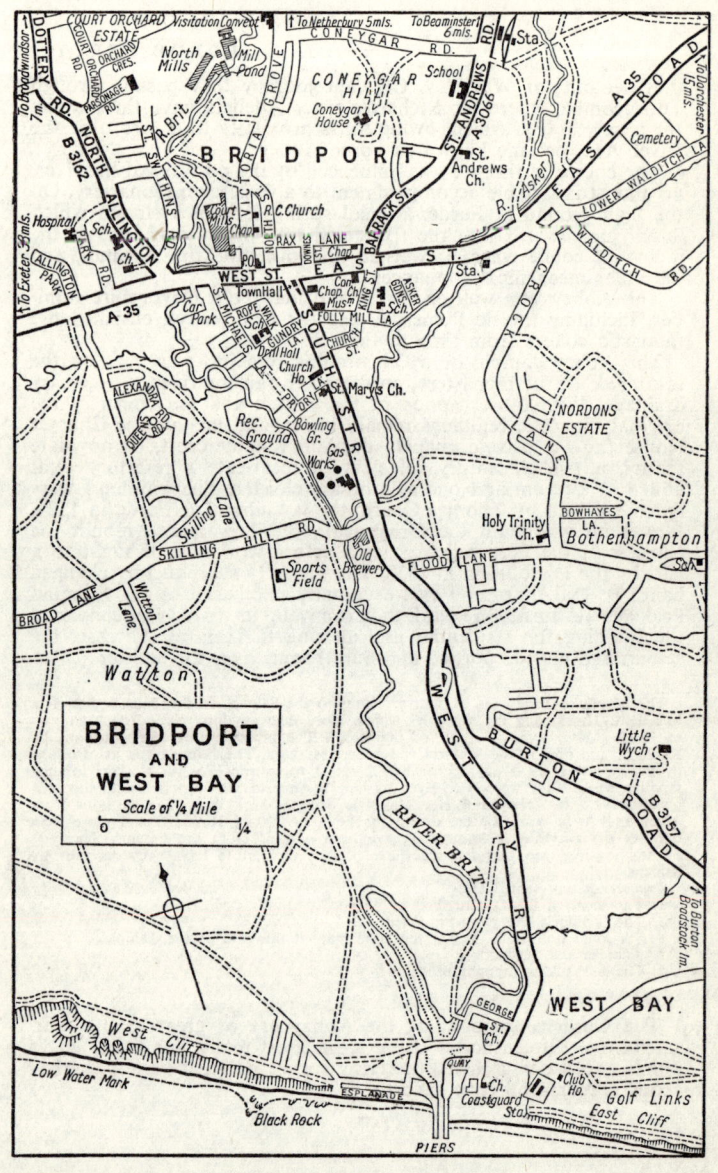

BRIDPORT
AND
WEST BAY

Scale of ¼ Mile

0   ¼

Bridport and West Bay

General Information

Access.—*By Rail:* From Paddington (149¼ m.), changing at Maiden Newton to local train for Bridport; or from Waterloo *via* Dorchester. Daily excursions throughout the season to the neighbouring resorts.

> *By Coach:* regular services from all parts.

> *By Road:* The trunk road A35 runs east and west through the town.

Banks.—*Lloyds*, West Street; *Barclays*, *Midland* and *Westminster*, East Street.

Buses.—To Lyme Regis and Axminster (*via* Chideock and Charmouth); Beaminster, West Bay, Crewkerne and Yeovil; Broadwindsor; Loders; Burton Bradstock; and Dorchester and Weymouth. For particulars *see* timetables.

Camping.—Municipal camping ground at West Bay. (Tel. 2424).

Car Parks.—West Street (also for coaches), East Street, South Street, and several at West Bay.

Churches and Chapels.

Parish Church (St. Mary's), South Street.
St. Andrew's, St. Andrew's Road.
St. Swithun's, Allington.
St. John's, West Bay.
Holy Trinity, Bothenhampton.
Roman Catholic (SS. Mary and Catherine), Victoria Grove.
Baptist, Victoria Grove.

Congregational, East Street.
Christian Science, Rax Lane.
Unitarian, East Street.
Methodist, South Street, and at West Bay in summer.
Society of Friends, South Street.

Coaches.—There are numerous trips to places of interest.

Early Closing.—Thursday.

Hotels.—*Greyhound*, East Street; *Knight's Bull*, East Street; *Crown*, West Bay Road; *Sun*, West Street; *George*, South Street; *Haydon Guest House*, West Allington.

Library.—Branch of County Library in East Street.

Market Days.—Wednesday and Saturday.

Municipal Art Gallery and Museum in South Street. Open mornings April-September.

Municipal Offices.—West Rivers, West Allington.

Museum.—South Street.

Population.—6,500.

Post Office.—West Street. Sub-offices at North Allington, West Bay, East Road and St. Andrew's Road.

Sport and Entertainment

Angling.—At West Bay from shore and boats. Competitions organized by *West Bay Sea Angling Club*, George Hotel, West Bay. Visitors are invited to compete.

Boating.—Boats can be hired for fishing, and sea- or river-trips.

Bowls.—Excellent green just behind St. Mary's Church in South Street.

Cinema.—*Palace*, South Street.

Cricket.—Ground is about half a mile from the town, just off the West Bay Road. Matches played throughout the season. Visitors welcomed. A Hockey Club uses the ground in winter.

Dances, etc.—At Masonic Hall, Colfox School Hall and Church House.

Golf.—*Bridport and West Dorset Golf Links* is a sporting course on East Cliff, West Bay.

Hunting.—The Cattistock Hunt meets in the neighbourhood during the season.

Music and Drama.—Local societies are active, viz. Bridport Amateur Operatic and Dramatic Society, Bridport and District Music Club, Bridport Choral Group.

Obstacle Golf.—At Municipal Camping Ground, West Bay.

Swimming.— *Bridport Swimming Club* holds galas and water polo matches at West Bay. No charge for swimming at West Bay.

Tennis.—Hard courts at rear of Municipal Offices.

The town of Bridport lies two miles inland from the sea and its offshoot, West Bay. A frequent service of buses links the two. The town is the Port Bredy of the novels of Thomas Hardy. The red-brick buildings and the generally warm colour of the place have a pleasing effect, enhanced by its wide main streets and a picturesque, wooded background. Bridport makes an excellent centre for exploring the attractions of West Dorset. Delightful rambles can be had in the neighbouring lanes and by-roads, and those who like longer excursions have a wide choice of objectives—commons and hill-tops, villages famous for their beauty or their associations, and old buildings of all kinds.

Bridport has many attractions, for its suburb, West Bay, is on the sea, with bathing, boating, water-polo and sea-fishing, while other facilities for sport include bowls, cricket, tennis, and an attractive golf course. Coaches make trips in the season, visiting well-known places both inland and on the coast.

Owing probably to its being the port of the river *Brit,* the town was of importance in Saxon days, although its early history is not of an engrossing kind, and it has never been distinguished by any really important event.

In the reign of Edward the Confessor the town could boast a mint, a priory of monks, and one hundred and twenty houses.

In the reign of Henry III it was a royal demesne, and this monarch made it a borough, although its charter underwent various alterations in subsequent reigns. The governing charter, prior to the Municipal Act, was granted by Charles II.

During the Civil War, the place was garrisoned alternately by Parliamentary and Royal troops, finally remaining with the former.

When Charles II arrived at Bridport in his hasty flight from Charmouth, the town was full of soldiers, part of an expedition about to sail for Jersey, but the royal party went boldly to an inn (the *George,* now a chemist's shop, incorporating part of the old building, opposite the Town Hall) and mixed with the company. Suspicion, however, was rife, so after a hasty meal Charles and his retinue quitted the town by the main road to Dorchester and took a lane leading to Broadwindsor, and so escaped Captain Macy, who, having failed to find his quarry at Bridport, had pushed on to the county town. **Lee Lane,** a mile east of Bridport (at the top of the hill beyond the level crossing) has been identified as the scene of this " Miraculous Divergence ", by which the proscribed prince escaped capture. A block of local grey stone at the junction of Lee Lane with the Dorchester road bears the following lines from Fuller's *Worthies*:

> " When 'midst your fiercest foes on every side,
> For your escape God did a Lane provide."

Unlike so many of the Stuart monarchs, Charles did not forget those, and they were many, who had befriended him; and on his coming to the throne in 1661, he granted pensions (in perpetuity) to his benefactors.

Marching from Lyme in 1685, Monmouth's troopers attacked the town, and two Dorsetmen were killed by the rebels, who, however, were quickly dispersed when the Dorset militia rallied their forces. By order of Jeffreys, twelve of the rebels were executed at Bridport.

Barrack Street was so named after the barracks of the garrison posted at Bridport when a French invasion was feared in George III's reign. The site is now occupied by the Port Bredy Hospital.

Although the Parish Church is the only ancient one now remaining, Bridport at one time possessed four others. St. Andrew's stood on the site now occupied by the Town Hall; St. John's where the Priory Mill (Youth Hostel) stands; St. Michael's by the lane of that name; and St. Swithun's by Allington Vicarage, the present church being on a different site. Other religious houses were St. John's Hospital on the town side of the East Bridge, and the Magdalen Leper House at Allington.

The rope-walks of Bridport were once a prominent feature, and in the surrounding fields the pretty blue-flowered flax was grown in enormous quantities. At one time the town enjoyed almost a monopoly in the manufacture of cordage for the navy. Gallows ropes were also made here, hence the grim retort often heard in "Wessex": "You'll live to be stabbed with a Bridport dagger!" The phrase misled the antiquary Leland, who, in his *Itinerary,* wrote of Bridport, "At Bridporth be made good daggers."

Most great industries leave their mark on the architecture of a town, and influence its planning. To this general rule Bridport is no exception, the great width of the streets being for the purpose of allowing each house to have a "rope-walk". Bridport is still the chief centre in Britain for the production of fishing nets, lines, twines and cordage. Modern factories and machinery have taken over much of the work formerly done by hand, but braiding, or the making of net, is still carried on in some homes.

From West Bay gravel has been exported for many years for various purposes, including water filtration. Agriculture and horticulture provide employment in the rural areas.

Other industries have developed in recent years, such as the manufacture of reinforced concrete units in the modern factory on West Bay Road.

The Parish Church

The Church of St. Mary is a fine Perpendicular building, cruciform in plan, with Early English transepts and an excellent central tower, capped with pinnacles and containing eight bells. The nave was lengthened by two bays when the church was "restored" in 1859-60. The bells were re-cast and re-hung in 1924, and at the same time a clock and chimes were added to the tower. The parvise chamber over the south porch has been opened into the church, and is used as a small gallery. Curious bosses will be noticed in the north transept, and another feature is the much-restored tomb of a cross-legged knight reputed to be a Crusader, John de Chideock. The register dates from 1600. St. Mary's was probably built about 1350, on the site of an older church, portions of which were used, there being traces of thirteenth-century work in the transepts.

Outside the western wall of the south porch is a solid block of freestone with a canopied niche in the centre, intended either for a figure of the Virgin, the dedicatory saint, or for some holy relic. That the niche was strongly guarded is apparent from the dowel holes still remaining, into which iron bars were leaded. Within two smaller niches on either side of the central one are effigies, but so worn that they cannot be identified. It has been conjectured that the stone may have once formed part of a shrine, reliquary, or cross.

The Seafront, Lyme Regis

Lyme Regis from the Cobb

West Bay

Weymouth and the Bay *(Valentine)*

A fine war memorial, designed by Sir Gilbert Scott, forms part of the boundary wall of the churchyard.

Opposite the Parish Church in South Street are some picturesque almshouses, given in 1696 by Daniel Taylor: they have recently been restored and accommodate about ten old folk.

Westward of St. Mary's Church are some fine playing fields of seven acres. Other recreation grounds are at Skilling Oval, Broadmead and Court Orchard.

The **Town Hall,** overlooking the cross-roads in the centre of the town, is a pleasing brick building of Georgian design faced with Portland stone erected in 1785-6. Inside are interesting mementoes; the walls are adorned with paintings—the work of a local artist—depicting incidents from the town's history. Visitors may see the interior on application at the Borough Offices, West Allington.

The **Museum and Art Gallery** (*open mornings, admission charge*) is in South Street in a Tudor-Gothic building with stone porch projecting on to the pavement, and formerly known as the Castle. There is an interesting collection of exhibits—paintings, ancient maps, antiquities discovered in the neighbourhood, and a natural history section. There are numerous exhibits recalling old industries including a " jumper " braiding loom still in working order.

Almost opposite the Museum in South Street are the **Borough Gardens.** These are tastefully laid out and may be reached from Gundry Lane, or through the Electricity Showroom.

Also in South Street, at its lower end on the west side, is the oldest building in the borough, called **The Chantry.** Little is known of its history, but it is thought from its design to have been the residence of the Prior.

Some excellent panelling, mantelpieces and carving remain in many of the houses hidden away in odd nooks and corners, familiar to local antiquaries, but not easily found by the tourist. The Liberal Hall in Barrack Street is now scheduled as an Ancient Monument.

The **Public Library,** a branch of the Dorset County Library, is in East Street, in the building formerly occupied by the Literary and Scientific Institute. It is open daily; it has lending and reference libraries, and provides study facilities.

Bridport was the birthplace of Bishop Giles, who covered the roof of his cathedral at Salisbury with lead, 700 years ago.

The celebrated historian, John Lothrop Motley, lived for some years in the home of his daughter at Kingston Russell, on the hills above the Bride Valley.

Captain Robert Kemball, the famous captain of the tea clipper, *Thermopylae*, lived in Bridport. His grave in the cemetery is marked by a Memorial Cross.

WEST BAY

Access.—Leave Bridport by South Street; in ½-mile fork right along West Bay Road. Frequent bus services from Bridport. Walkers can go by field-path behind St. Mary's Church.
Churches.—St. John's (*H.C.* 9 a.m.), 8 p.m.; *Methodist*, 11.

Hotels.—*George, Bridport Arms, Haddon House, West Bay, The Moorings,* etc.
Post Office.—Over footbridge opposite George Hotel.
Municipal Camping Ground.—Apply to Camp Supervisor, West Bay. (Tel. Bridport 2424).

The quaint harbour and holiday resort of West Bay lies about 1½ miles south of Bridport. The real and original name for the place is Bridport Harbour or Quay, and it is only in comparatively recent years that the inappropriate name of West Bay has been bestowed upon it.

Though a small resort it is popular, particularly with campers and caravaners, there being a well organized municipal camping ground. Separate chalets are also available for renting. Close to this ground is a pavilion with facilities for games and dancing. Free bathing can be enjoyed from an extensive pebble beach. Good sea fishing, boating and sailing is available, and galas and water polo are frequently arranged. Golf links are on East Cliff and cricket is played at West Bay road. The Esplanade is a popular promenade giving fine views seaward. This part is now being rapidly developed with chalets, a motel and shopping precinct.

The **Harbour** with its wide quays and jumble of boats and nets is situated at the mouth of the river, which is tidal for about a mile but not now navigable for ships. The opening between the cliffs is less than 600 yards in width, the excavated harbour basin being midway.

Excursions from Bridport

TO EYPE AND CHIDEOCK

Most visitors find their way westward along the cliffs to—

Eype

where the broken cliffs, the beach, and the extensive upland common provide many quiet spots for all who like to spend lazy days. It may be reached direct from Bridport by a delightful ramble across fields by way of Allington, the Lovers' Grove, and field-path to Eype church, standing on the ridge, whence the rough lane leads through the village, down a ravine to the beach; but perhaps the best way is by the path starting from West Bay and running not far from the edge of the cliff. The slipping nature of the coast hereabouts has necessitated considerable sloping off and draining and the building of a sea wall. Several paths cross inland over Eype Down, which has an interesting earthwork.

Continuing over Thorncombe Beacon we reach **Seatown** (*Anchor Inn*), a little settlement in a more open situation than Eype, in the next break in the cliffs. It is a seaside offshoot of Chideock, a mile inland on the Lyme Regis road. Seatown, like all these places where a house or two may be found in a break in the cliffs, is growing in a modest way, with a few boats, the inevitable huts, and facilities for refreshment.

Chideock

Chideock (*The George Inn*), about 3 miles west of Bridport, is an attractive village, with picturesque cottages built in local sandstone. The name is pronounced *Chiddick*. The old lords of the manor were the de Chideocks, whose castle, built by John de Chideock in 1379, was laid in ruins after the great Rebellion by Colonel Ceeley, Governor of Lyme. Only part of the moat remains, although considerable portions of the castle were standing so late as 1733, when Buck published a view of them. The site of the castle is in a field to the north-east of the church.

The **Church,** mainly of the Perpendicular period, suffered considerable damage during the Civil War and was well restored in 1884. At the east end of the south aisle is the historic Arundell Chapel with the black marble tomb of Sir John Arundell *circa* 1515, and on it lies the effigy of the knight, in complete plate armour. This Sir John was knighted for his valour at the Battles of Terouen and Tournay in 1514. His eldest son, another Sir John, resided at Chideock Castle, and was the ancestor of the Arundels of Lanherne, Cornwall; his second son, Sir Thomas, married Margaret Howard, sister of Katharine, fifth wife of Henry VIII. Accused of being an accomplice in the Duke of Somerset's plot that led to the murder of John Dudley, Duke of Northumberland, he was beheaded February 26, 1552. Sir Matthew, son of Sir Thomas, was the ancestor of the famous Lords Arundel of Wardour, Wiltshire.

In the **Manor House** grounds is a highly ornamental Roman Catholic Chapel with some valuable frescoes. The Roman Catholic cemetery, by the parish churchyard, has a chapel containing a number of mural paintings.

The return to Bridport can be made either direct by the main road, or by path and lane through—

Symondsbury

which lies to the north. This village is prettily situated in a secluded and well-wooded hollow. The *Ilchester Arms* is an ancient thatched inn. The church, mainly Perpendicular, has a slightly tapering tower. Galston, Bishop of Bristol, and uncle of Joseph Addison, is buried in the church. The village lies at the foot of a striking conical eminence called **Colmer's Hill,** and looking seawards Golden Cap and Eype Down are prominent. On regaining the high road, by keeping to the right beyond the church Bridport is soon reached, an alternative and shorter route being by a path which will be noticed next to the entrance lane to a farm at the foot of a hill at the end of the village. The enterprising will find longer paths and lanes round or over **Allington Hill.**

TO WHITCHURCH CANONICORUM AND LAMBERT'S CASTLE

The route from Bridport is by way of Chideock and More-combelake, turning inland, crossing the Char below Whitchurch, and going right at Baker's Cross. (Motorists should be prepared for one or two steep hills after leaving the main road at More-combelake for the narrower lane across the Vale.) Many will prefer to follow the main road to Charmouth and *Hunter's Lodge Inn*, where turn right for the Castle, returning *via* Marshwood and Broadwindsor. Walkers can return *via Hunter's Lodge Inn* or *via* Charmouth.

Whitchurch Canonicorum

The delightful village of Whitchurch Canonicorum in Marshwood Vale is one of the largest parishes in the county. The name is derived from St. Wite (or Wita) which name the Normans took to mean White, and which they latinized in St.

Candida, the patron saint. *Canonicorum* was added after 1242 when the Canons of Wells and Sarum appropriated the greater tithes. So it became the *White Church of the Canons*.

The **Church** is interesting, cruciform in plan, and with a western tower. There are few traces of the Saxon church which originally

38

occupied the site, to be followed by the Norman church. The present building was erected early in the thirteenth century, and incorporated part of this Norman church. It is dedicated to the Holy Cross and St. Candida, and was part restored in 1849. The south doorway is a fine example of Transition-Norman, the chancel and a portion of the nave belonging to the same period, i.e. about 1150. The transepts and chancel were built about 1200, and the tower and oak roof about 1400. The font is coeval with the south doorway. Above the shrine of St. Candida is a Perpendicular window of three lights. The church has much interesting detail for the archaeologist.

The shrine and tomb of St. Candida are in the north transept. It is interesting as being the only shrine remaining in England, with the exception of those of Edward the Confessor in Westminster Abbey and of Thomas à Becket in Canterbury. Beneath the tomb are three oval openings in which small articles and offerings may be placed to become endowed with healing virtues.

Other monuments include those to Sir John Jefferey, of Catherstone, *obiit* 1611, and to John Wadham (d. 1584), Recorder of Lyme, and for some time Captain of Sandsfoot Castle, near Weymouth. On the wall of the chancel is a modern brass commemorating Sir George Somers, discoverer of the Bermudas. High up on the outside walls of the tower are several carved panels which may have come from the Saxon church, and the porch has some well-carved gargoyles of fifteenth-century date.

For **Lambert's Castle** *see* p. 22.

TO BRADPOLE AND LODERS

A pretty circular excursion of 5 or 6 miles embraces these places. Turn out of East Street just beyond the Library and follow the Beaminster road (bus route) for a mile to a right turning at the *Kings Head Inn* for **Bradpole** a pleasant little village with a church erected in 1845 on the site of two earlier buildings. It possesses a beautiful sixteenth-century communion cup. The Memorial Hall commemorates *W. E. Forster*, the statesman mainly responsible for the Elementary Education Act of 1870, which made education accessible to all children.

Eastward of Bradpole, housing development almost joins it with **Loders** an attractive little village with several pretty cottages and an inn, *The Farmers' Arms.* Overlooking it are several tor-like hills crowned with firs. **Uploders,** or more correctly *Upper Loders*, forms the eastern end.

The **Church,** of charmingly lichened brown stone and dedicated to St. Mary Magdalene, is very interesting. It is mainly Perpendicular, and when it was restored several years ago, a Norman window and doorway in the chancel were opened up, and an Easter sepulchre and hagioscope discovered. There are two empty niches and a headless cross in the south aisle, which was evidently a chapel, as there is also a piscina. There is a priest's chamber over the porch, approached from the interior by a staircase in an octagonal turret. It seems to have had also a screen, the stairs to the loft being used for the pulpit. There is also a rare, old oak Parish chest, with beautifully carved panels dating from the fourteenth century.

Loders was once the seat of a Benedictine Priory, founded by Baldwin de Redvers in the reign of Henry I. It became a cell to the Abbey of Montebourg, near Coutances, to which it and the church and manor of Axmouth were granted by Richard de Redvers. It is said that the making of wine from apples—now known as cider—was introduced into Dorset by the monks.

An excellent extension of this excursion is to pretty little **Askerswell** and the finely situated camp on **Eggardon Hill,** over 800 feet above the sea and with correspondingly wide views. The camp bears a strong resemblance to the more famous Maiden Castle, near Dorchester, and the comparison has suggested to many the very excellent walk along the old Roman road from Eggardon to Dorchester.

TO BEAMINSTER AND BROADWINDSOR

No visitor to Bridport should miss Beaminster, 6 miles to the north, easily reached by road (bus service).

For Walkers. The main road is apt to be too busy with traffic for pleasurable walking. A somewhat preferable route begins by the turning on the north side of West Street near the Post Office. Beyond Pymore Mills, where lane turns to cross river, take path along east bank of stream; or follow lane as it rambles along the western bank by Elwell and Waytown to **Netherbury,** charmingly placed. The church on the hillside dates from *c.* 1350, and contains many interesting features—including a twelfth-century font, and Elizabethan pulpit with inlaid oak panels. From Netherbury a footpath leads in less than 2 miles to **Beaminster.** The main road passes the little village of **Melplash,** where is the interesting Tudor House of **Melplash Court.** It was the ancient seat of the More family, and came by marriage to the Paulets, whose coat-of-arms and motto over the hall chimney-piece were removed to Mapperton. In the grounds are a fine barn and circular pigeon-house.

Beaminster

Beaminster (*White Hart*), in the midst of a rich agricultural district, is one of the most delightful towns in West Dorset. It is a typical thriving country town, with streets radiating from the market square. Here, close to the site of the old cross taken down about 1750, is the modern *Market Cross.* Londoners will be interested to know that the pinnacles, of Portland stone, came from Christ's Hospital when it was demolished to make way for the General Post Office in Newgate Street.

Beaminster is of considerable antiquity. At the time of the Domesday Survey the manor belonged to the see of Salisbury, and in 1091 it was given by Bishop Osmund to augment two of the Cathedral prebends. On Palm Sunday, 1644, Prince Maurice was quartered here, but did not remain long as, in a fire which broke out—its cause being disputed—the town was nearly burned to the ground. In the following year Sprigge passed through with Fairfax's army, when the town presented "the pittyfullest Spectacle that Man can behold, hardly an house left not consumed". Other conflagrations took place in 1684 and 1781. Consequently, Beaminster today has many picturesque but few really old houses, although much ancient stone-work and carving is hidden behind comparatively modern walls. Fortunately its fine church never suffered. Beaminster was formerly a flax growing centre. The terraces or "lynchets" on the surrounding hills were used for drying the flax.

The **Church** is approached by a road at the corner of the market place. Externally Perpendicular, it is one of the best in Dorset, and has a tower not unworthy to rank with that fine group which give architectural distinction to the neighbouring county of Somerset. The interior consists of a nave of five bays, chancel, aisles, and north porch. The steps and doorway that led to the old rood-loft remain in the south aisle, but the present screen is modern. The nave, arcade and a squint from the south aisle into the chancel are Early English. The pulpit is Jacobean. The chancel screen is modern, but the zigzag mouldings outside the chancel door, and the square font bowl on a modern base, were in the original Norman church and date from the twelfth century. There are two pompous monuments to members of the Strode family, and some memorial win-

41

dows to the Oglanders and other benefactors. The north chapel was built by John Hillary, of Meerhay, in 1505, and " beautified by Mrs. Mary Mills of Meerhay in 1767 ". There are a number of brasses in the church, the earliest bearing date 1591. A curious little building, known as the *Mort House*, once adjacent to the church, has now been incorporated in the building, and forms a vestry.

The tower of the church is built of warm-coloured Ham Hill stone, and dates from the early years of the sixteenth century. It is a highly ornamental piece of work, and is adorned with thirty-eight crocketed pinnacles, placed at effective points. Here also are sculptured representations of the Crucifixion, the Virgin, the Resurrection and the Ascension and of St. George slaying the dragon. The canopied niches, containing figures, hollowed out of the faces of the buttresses, are extremely beautiful, as also are the bands of carved quatrefoils. The gilded weather-vane is of seventeenth- or eighteenth-century date.

Almost hidden by the high ground of the churchyard is a charming little **Almshouse,** erected and endowed in 1630 by Sir John Strode, of Parnham, on the site of an ancient chantry house. A mile south is **Parnham House** of Tudor date (*open Thursday afternoons, May–September*).

About 2 miles from Beaminster by way of Storridge Hill and to the right past Marsh Farm, is **Mapperton,** an interesting old manor house. Only the north wing remains, a fine Tudor fragment with Jacobean additions, and possessing some good ceilings, Italian in style. The front of the house is enclosed by a low wall and rails, in the centre of which are gates, whose posts carry griffins, the crest of the Morgan family. Near by is the stone church dating from 1704 which possesses some very fine glass, heraldic and pictorial. The original village of Mapperton was wiped out in 1666 during the Great Plague.

The return to Bridport may well be made *via* Broadwindsor, less than 3 miles westward by the main road. A preferable route, however, is through **Stoke Abbot,** of which village the poet Crowe was rector. The village is charmingly situated amongst deeply sunk lanes, and contains some picturesque old houses, some of which date from early in the seventeenth century. The Church was partially rebuilt in 1828, when the tower was struck by lightning, the restoration being completed in 1878. Its most ancient remaining features are a good Norman font and a seventeenth-century pulpit. The lane climbing the hillside just below the church approach is the shortest route to Lewesdon and the Broadwindsor road. Alternatively motorists can go right through the village and get up to the main road by a slightly longer, but very pretty, route.

Broadwindsor

is the third largest parish in the diocese of Salisbury. A bus runs from Bridport. It was to this village that Charles II and his retinue made their way after the "miraculous divergence", staying at the George Inn of that time. A commemorative tablet has been placed on the wall of a house which may possibly have formed part of the original inn. From Trent House Charles eventually made his way to Shoreham, in Sussex, where he took ship to Fécamp.

The **Church** was almost entirely rebuilt in 1868. The original design was followed, and among the old portions retained was the fine Jacobean pulpit used by Thomas Fuller. Apart from its historical associations, this is one of the best Jacobean pulpits remaining in Dorset. Fuller's best-known work, *The Worthies of England*, was published the year after his death in 1661. During recent restoration it was revealed that three of the church bells are very ancient and valuable, having been cast, it is thought, in the thirteenth century. The Vicarage, possibly once the Manor House, dates in part from 1700.

Very prominent landmarks of the Beaminster district are **Pilsdon Pen** (909 ft.) and **Lewesdon Hill** (894 ft.), now National Trust, which are close to Broadwindsor, and are known locally as the "Cow and Calf". On the north-west slope of Pilsdon is **Racedown Lodge,** said to be the Kullynch Hall or Uppercross of *Persuasion*, for two years the home of Wordsworth and his sister Dorothy. On this hill also is an ancient camp with strong ramparts and ditches.

The village of **Pilsdon,** 5 miles west of Beaminster, and 7 from Bridport, was the birthplace of Sir John Hody, Chief Justice of the King's Bench in 1440, and of other distinguished members of the same family. The church of St. Mary was so thoroughly restored in 1830 that it has retained few ancient features, excepting a good piscina and a stoup in the porch. The western bell turret was erected in 1865.

TO BURTON BRADSTOCK

A pleasant coast walk from Bridport or West Bay is to **Burton Bradstock,** some three miles to the south-east of Bridport, a very pretty village (*Anchor Inn, Three Horseshoes Inn* (teas)) close to the mouth of the River Bride, or Bredy. It may be reached by road (bus service), passing **Bothenhampton** on the way and pausing to admire the ancient church with its 800-year-old font, or by a fine cliff walk from West Bay over the golf links. It is a charming village with interesting houses and attractive surroundings. The first half of the name is from Brideton, the second half from Bradenstock, to which Wiltshire abbey it once belonged.

There are good bathing and fishing facilities from the beach of fine shingle. Its neighbour, **Burton Freshwater,** half a mile westward, is popular for picnics (caravan site).

Burton Bradstock **Church** is an old cruciform building, chiefly Perpendicular, with an embattled central Tower. The Jacobean communion rails carry the date 1686. The pulpit is of oak. A rather curious painted panelling covers the lower part of the wall; an inscription along the top and ending by the pulpit sets forth the dates of the original building and later repairs. Note the entrance to the rood-loft. The clock came from Christ's Hospital, London.

At **Burton Cliff** really commences the famous ridge of pebbles known as **The Chesil Beach** although this tails off from West Bay in the form of fine shingle. The Beach continues to Portland, a distance of eighteen miles. For a description, *see* p. 62.

This walk may be continued in an easterly direction to **Swyre,** lying between Puncknowle Knoll and Beacon Knap, and on past the embryo resort rather ambitiously known as **Bexington-on-Sea** and so to **Abbotsbury.** (*See* p. 71.)

Just before reaching Swyre a lane to the left passes *Berwick Farm,* the birthplace of John Russell, the founder of the ducal House of Bedford. The house, although modernized, has retained portions of the old chapel and some fine oak beams.

Almost opposite the house a field-path across the little river *Bride* leads to **Chilcombe,** a tiny village of cottages and small Manor-House.

Returning to the main road a right-hand turn takes us to **Puncknowle** (pronounced *Punnell*), with a charming Jacobean *Manor House* and some picturesque cottages. The church has extensive remains of Norman work. There are various memorials to the Napier family—who owned Puncknowle Manor—and an unusual font.

From Puncknowle a short walk leads to **Swyre** on the small Dorset estate of the Duke of Bedford. The church, dating from 1505, was largely rebuilt in 1863.

Weymouth

Angling.—Excellent from both boats and the shore. Motor boats leave the quays at advertised times for mackerel fishing, line and bait being provided. The *Weymouth Angling Society* hold a four-days' festival in September and foreshore and boat competitions are held during the season. The Weymouth Corporation hold an International Sea Angling Festival in September or October. The variety of fish caught is exceptional and semi-tropical specimens are often present in the sheltered bay.

Banks.—*Lloyds, Westminster, National Provincial* and *Wessex Trustee Savings Bank* in St. Thomas Street; *Barclays* and *Midland* in St. Mary Street.

Bathing.—The sands are smooth, firm, and reasonably safe, there being no current nor any hidden rocks anywhere on the beach. Between the Clock and the pier the slope is gentle and it is necessary to go some distance out for deep water. Towards the north end a fringe of shingle skirts the promenade and the slope is steeper. There are good changing facilities and several rafts are anchored in the bay.

There is bathing from the Pier, where Weymouth Swimming Club welcome visitors and hold galas and competitions.

Boating.—Skiffs, rowing boats, canoes, floats and pedaloes are available for hire on the seafront, and larger sailing boats in the harbour. The bay is one of the best sailing grounds in England. The *Royal Dorset Yacht Club* and *Town Regattas* are usually held in August, just after Cowes Week, and many of the large yachts compete.

The *Royal Dorset Yacht Club* has a comfortable clubhouse on the Esplanade. The *Weymouth Sailing Club*, Nothe Pier, and the *Castle Cove Sailing Club*, Old Castle Road, hold races in the bay and Portland Roads respectively.

Bowls.—Fine green in Greenhill Gardens, where *Greenhill Bowling Club* has headquarters. Visitors' competitions during the season and open tournament during first week of September.

There is a public green in Melcombe Regis Gardens.

Buses.—There are frequent services between—

Weymouth, Wyke Regis and Portland (Victoria Square and Southwell). Some buses go on to Portland Bill.

,,   Chickerell, Langton Herring, Portesham and Abbotsbury.
,,   and Westham.
,,   Preston, Sutton Poyntz and Osmington Mills.
,,   Radipole and Upwey Wishing Well.

There are services two or three times a day from Bournemouth through Dorchester and Weymouth to Portland, from Weymouth to Wareham, Corfe and Swanage, from Weymouth through Dorchester or Abbotsbury to Bridport.

Coaches run daily between Weymouth and Victoria Coach Station during the season. Daily services are operated by South-Western bus companies to Salisbury, Lyme Regis, Sidmouth, Seaton, and Exeter, and there are through services to South Wales, the Midlands and the North. All long-distance services start from the Coach Station, off King Street, near the main railway station. Approximate time for journeys: London 7 hours; Birmingham 8 hours; Manchester 12 hours.

Churches and Chapels.—

St. Mary's (Parish Church of Melcombe Regis), St. Mary Street.
Holy Trinity, Town Bridge.
St. Nicholas, Buxton Road.
St. John's, Esplanade.
St. Paul's, Abbotsbury Road.
St. Anne's, Radipole.
St. Aldhelm's, Spa Road, Radipole.
All Saints', Wyke Regis.
St. Laurence's, Upwey.
St. Andrew's, Preston.
St. Nicholas, Broadwey.
St. Edmund of Canterbury, Lanehouse Rocks Road, Weymouth.
Roman Catholic: St. Augustine's, Dorchester Road; *St. Joseph's,* Westham Road.
Congregational: Gloucester Street; Roman Road, Radipole; Hope Square; Upwey.
Methodist: Maiden Street; St. Leonard's Road; Derby Street; Broadwey; Elwell Street, Upwey; Newstead Road, Westham; Portland Road, Wyke Regis.
Baptist, Bank Buildings, Esplanade.
Christian Scientist, Melcombe Avenue.
Salvation Army, Citadel, Westham Road.
Gospel Hall, Turton Street; *Bethany Hall,* Westham Road.
Ebenezer Hall, Abbotsbury Road.
Society of Friends, Lower Bond Street Hall.
National Spiritualist Mission, Lower Bond Street Hall.

Cinemas.—*Gaumont,* St. Thomas Street; *Classic,* Gloucester Street.

Climate.—Weymouth's record of low rainfall and brilliant sunshine is one of the best among South Coast resorts. The crescent of the bay makes a good suntrap, the Downs sheltering it from cold north winds.

Clubs, etc.—Royal Dorset Yacht Club, on the Esplanade, **Conservative,** King's Street; **Rotary,** luncheons at Gloucester Hotel; **Masonic Hall,** St. Thomas Street; Weymouth Branch of the **British Legion** is in Westwey Road, where newspapers and games are provided and ex-Servicemen welcomed; **Toc H** meet at Talbot House, 26 Ranelagh Road. The **Weymouth and South Dorset Arts Centre,** which houses and encourages cultural societies and activities of all kinds, is in Commercial Road. There

46

are flourishing Clubs for Cricket, Association and Rugby Football, Boxing, Archery, Sailing, Swimming, Chess, Shooting and Dramatics. There are also several Riding Establishments in the neighbourhood. Details of all these may be had from the **Information Centre** on the Esplanade, where all enquiries about the town and district are answered gratis.

Distances.—

	Miles.		Miles.		Miles.
Abbotsbury	9	Lulworth Cove	14	Radipole	2½
Bournemouth	31	Maiden Castle	6¼	Sandsfoot Castle	1¼
Bridport	19	Nothe Point	1¼	Sherborne	26
Came Down		Osmington Mills	6	Swanage (road)	27
(Golf Links)	6½	Poole	30	Upwey Well	4
Cerne Abbas	16	Portesham	7½	Wareham	19
Chickerell Links	2	Portland Station	4½	Westham	½
Corfe Castle	22	Pier Head	¾	Wool	14
Dorchester	8	Preston	3¼	Wyke Regis	1¼

Early Closing.—Wednesday.

Entertainments.—Summer shows at the Pavilion. Dancing at *Pavilion Ballroom.*

Golf.—The **Weymouth Golf Links** (18 holes), property of the Corporation, lie between West Bay and Weymouth Bay, within a mile of the open sea on either side, and about a mile from the King's Statue. Frequent bus service. Sunday play and medal competitions monthly. Refreshments.

The **Came Down Golf Club** (18 holes) on Came Down midway between Weymouth and Dorchester is available to visitors on application to the Secretary. It is reached by bus from Weymouth or Dorchester to Herringstone turn, then a walk of one mile through the park. Resident steward and stewardess.

Putting greens in Greenhill Gardens; Melcombe Regis Gardens; Home Close Gardens, Wyke Regis; and in Overcombe Park.

Greyhound Racing.—Frequent meetings at Wessex Stadium, Radipole Lane, where also motor racing and track events are sometimes held.

Hotels.—*Royal*, Esplanade; *Gloucester*, Esplanade; *Crown*, St. Thomas Street; *Lupins*, Greenhill; *Trelawney*, Old Castle Road; *Oxford*, Esplanade; *Edward*, Alexander Gardens; *Clifton*, Queen Street; *Rodwell*, Rodwell Road; *Grand*, Esplanade; *Greenhill*, Greenhill; *Russell*, Esplanade; *Fairhaven*, Esplanade; *Cavendish*, Esplanade; *Leam*, Royal Crescent; *Crescent*, Esplanade; *Alexandra*, Esplanade; *Fedora*, Esplanade; *Windsor*, Dorchester Road; *Mon Ami*, Esplanade; *Burdon*, Esplanade; *Strathmore*, Esplanade; *Burlington*, Esplanade; *Allenby*, Dorchester Road; *Esplanade*, Royal Terrace; *Rosedene Guest House*, Carlton Road North; *Westfield Guest House*, Kirtleton Avenue.

Camps: *Riviera Holiday Hotel* (Pontins), Bowleaze Cove; *Pontins Chalet Holiday Camp*, Osmington; *Chesil Beach Holiday Camp*, Wyke Regis; *Sea View Caravan Camp*, Preston.

Information Centre.—Esplanade.

Library.—In Westwey Road, at end of Westham Bridge.

Population.—42,160.

Post Office.—Chief office is in St. Thomas Street.

Railway stations.—King Street, close to Clock Tower. The former branch line to Portland is closed. Boat trains run round the back of the town to the pier.

Sea Trips.—British Rail vessels, local steamers and launches provide a great variety of excursions including those to Portland Bill, Shambles Lightship, Lulworth Cove, Swanage, Bournemouth, Isle of Wight, and across channel to Cherbourg. There are occasional trips to H.M. Ships and Portland Harbour. A fine though sometimes rough sea voyage is to the Channel Islands.

Tennis.—Numerous courts in Greenhill Gardens, Radipole Park, Melcombe Regis Gardens, and Wyke Regis Gardens. There are several clubs at which visitors are welcome.

Theatre.—Pavilion Theatre, southern end of Esplanade, near harbour.

Strictly speaking, *Weymouth* is only a tiny old seaport fringed with newer houses, on the right bank of the little river *Wey*, while the bigger, more bustling seaside town which is strung out along the bay, northward from the left bank, is *Melcombe* —originally called after an ancient mill, long since disappeared —with *" Regis "* added to indicate that it formed part of a royal domain.

For the sake of convenience, however, and following popular custom, the name Weymouth is used alone whenever reference is made in these pages to the conjoined towns of Weymouth and Melcombe Regis.

The chief natural attraction of the place is undoubtedly its glorious bay, which, for brilliance of colour and grace of line, is without a rival on the south coast. With a fairly wide open curve on the north and a narrow sharper curve on the south, the bay is nearly five miles across, and about two and a half miles in depth from north to south.

The town is built along this extended frontage, and for the most part faces east, lying open to the fresh breezes from the Channel, but protected from the north and east winds by

Osmington Mills   (*Valentine*)

Chesil Beach and Portland Harbour   (*Etches*)

Portland Bill (*Gerald Wilson*)

Cerne Abbas (*J. Scheerboom*)

the long line of the Purbeck Hills, which stretch eastward from the north end of the beautiful crescent and terminate abruptly in the picturesque cliffs of St. Aldhelm's Head.

In the west, Chesil Beach, the most dangerous on the south coast, stretches from Bridport to Portland, which it joins to the mainland, thus protecting Weymouth Bay from south-west gales. In its dull monotony of pebble ridge it bears eloquent testimony to the strength of Channel winds and currents.

There is comparatively little depth to the town, the western portion being confined by the outflow of the River Wey, formerly called the Backwater. This is now, as **Radipole Lake**, the home of a Swannery, and the surrounding land has been largely reclaimed and attractively laid out, though its influence still persists in shaping the residential part of the town. Across Radipole Lake the industrial suburb of **Westham** has developed rapidly within recent years, tapering out along the Chickerell Road, while modern growth is also responsible for the incorporation of such pleasant districts as **Bincleaves** and **Rodwell** on the hilly ground west of the harbour. The marsh of Lodmoor, once an arm of the sea, has channelled new development on the Melcombe side along the line of the Dorchester Road. The villages of Broadwey and Upwey are now linked to the town by a continuous residential area.

The shopping and business centres of the town are **St. Thomas Street** and **St. Mary Street**, between the Harbour and the King's Statue. The Esplanade, which they join at this point, curves round to the Pier, the triangular space between it and the straight streets being filled up with quaint wedges of houses and narrow little cross alleys, which will scarcely carry more than one car at a time.

It may be stated at once that Weymouth owes its charm chiefly to situation and climate, and not to architectural achievements, for it has scarcely any large buildings calling for description, though some of the little bow-fronted houses with their delicate iron balconies give an impression of the demure gaiety of Jane Austen which is quite delightful, and round the quay are winding streets, tiny old inns, ships' chandlers' shops and all the other eternal fascinations of an ancient fishing port.

Weymouth is now first and foremost a seaside resort, with wonderful sands, good water supply and a splendid climate. It is within easy reach of London and the Midlands, and although its most important season is the summer, its natural advantages of climate and position make it admirably adapted for winter holidaying or permanent residence.

Although catering for visitors is the most important occupation, there are flourishing industries as well, such as brewing, sail-making, shipbuilding, and light engineering. Weymouth has a large trade with the Channel Islands, exporting corn and importing large quantities of fruit and tomatoes.

Antiquities

The town itself is not very rich in relics of ancient times, and has scarcely any buildings of an earlier date than the eighteenth century. But Radipole was a port in Roman times, and the surrounding hills are covered with an almost incredible number of barrows, tumuli and cromlechs carrying us back in thought to the misty past when man's chief concern, after providing for present needs, was to perpetuate the memory of the dead and ensure a safe journey to the shades.

Near the town are the Roman tessellated pavement and temple at Preston; Sandsfoot Castle, with Portland Castle opposite, and the wonderful earthworks of Maiden Castle and Chalbury Camp, all of which are described elsewhere in this book (*see* Index).

The most ancient buildings actually in the town are the **Old Assembly Rooms** in Cove Street, Old Weymouth—now the back entrance to an inn—and a building in Maiden Street; where a cannon ball embedded in the gable end recalls one of the incidents of the Civil War. In Trinity Street is one of the few remaining Tudor houses. This has some of the original glass in its mullioned windows, twin gables and a stone slab roof.

Near the Clock Tower and almost adjoining the *Royal Hotel* is the older and historic *Gloucester Hotel*, for several summers a favourite residence of George III.

One or two of the churches contain old paintings and other

objects of interest, while in the **Guildhall** are preserved a chest captured from a ship of the Spanish Armada, now used to store the Corporation Insignia; an ancient chair from the old Friary that formerly stood near; the old stocks and whipping post; portraits of the Duke of Wellington, George III, and Sir Christopher Wren; and some fine old oak carving of the period of James I.

St. Mary's Church is a rectangular building of stone erected on the site of a former church, and opened in 1817. It is finely proportioned and the interior is decorated in the best style of tne period. At the east end is a famous painting of "The Last Supper," by *Sir James Thornhill* (1675–1734), who was born at Weymouth and represented the borough in Parliament. It may be remembered that he was responsible for the eight paintings, representing scenes from the life of St. Paul, with which the interior dome of St. Paul's Cathedral is decorated.

On a slab outside St. Mary's Schools may be seen inscribed George the Third's pious sentiment: "It is my wish that every child in my kingdom should be able to read the Bible."

Holy Trinity Church, facing the south end of the Town Bridge, is one of the finest buildings in old Weymouth, or Weymouth proper. It was erected in 1836 and enlarged in 1887. In the Lady Chapel is a painting of the Crucifixion, attributed to the school of Van Dyck.

Parks and Gardens

Greenhill Gardens are close to the sea at the northern end of the Esplanade. On rising ground, they have a lovely view seawards, and form a quiet and pleasant retreat. There are excellent tennis courts, bowling and putting greens, a refreshment kiosk and a most attractive floral clock, which is floodlit on summer evenings.

Melcombe Regis Gardens, stretching along the water-side from Westham Bridge to Melcombe Regis Station, form part of the Corporation's scheme for reclaiming and beautifying the back of the town. They contain a Palm House, Rose Walk, tennis courts and putting and bowling greens.

The **Nothe Gardens** are prettily laid-out shady walks, with magnificent views above the Nothe Parade, on the south side of the Harbour. The Municipality, under the direction of a well-known landscape artist, has further developed and beautified these gardens. The same artist has laid out the grounds round **Sandsfoot Castle** as a charmingly formal Tudor Garden.

For **Radipole Park** and **Lake** *see* p. 54.

Public Buildings

The **Town Bridge,** opened in 1930 by King George VI when Duke of York, replaced a swing bridge constucted in 1824. It is built of steel and concrete, and its two leaves, electrically operated, can open and shut in two or three minutes. In the western parapet is a large block of granite engraved " From Weymouth in New England to Weymouth in Old England."

The **Esplanade,** about a mile long, follows the curve of the bay from Greenhill Gardens in the north round to the Stone Pier in the south. It is well provided with seats and pleasant shelters, with a bandstand towards the northern end. Coloured illuminations at night produce a most pleasing effect reflected in the waters of the Bay. The **Clock Tower** in the centre is a useful landmark. (*See* p. 55.)

The **Guildhall,** built in the Grecian style in 1836 on the site of the original Melcombe Guildhall, stands at the junction of Edmund Street and the southern end of St. Mary Street. The ground floor is used as a Police Station, while above are the police court and civic chamber. Over the Mayoral Chair is a fine piece of oak carving bearing the date 1577, brought from the church which preceded the present St. Mary's.

The **Municipal Offices** are housed opposite the Alexandra Gardens, at the corner of Belle Vue.

The Piers, Harbour and Nothe

The old Pier used to be called the Pile Pier to distinguish it from the Stone or South Pier on the opposite side of the Harbour. It too has now been reconstructed in stone. At the shore end stands the modern Weymouth Pavilion, the latest entertainment and social centre of the town. The Pavilion incorporates a ballroom, theatre, restaurant and bars. On the south side are platforms, customs sheds and refreshment rooms for the Channel Islands and other passengers. On the north side are a promenade, dressing-cubicles and diving stage, with a café at the end. Weymouth Swimming Club holds gala nights once each week during the summer season. There are water-polo matches off the end of the Pier, and free fishing.

Close to the pier gates is a *Ferry* (rowing boat) across to the **Nothe,** a headland terminating in a fort and a stone pier, one of the favourite haunts of sea-anglers. This can be reached by car from the Town Bridge. It is much better, however, to explore the Nothe on foot, as the gradients are very steep and the best viewpoints are gained up little flights of steps. The Nothe Gardens are, of course, closed to cars. The headland and its pier together form the southern arm of the Harbour.

The view from the top of the Nothe is magnificent, and the sight of Portland in the early morning will not quickly be forgotten. Below the dismantled Verne Citadel which crowns the Portland cliffs is a gigantic Breakwater, which cost over £1,000,000, and forms one of the principal arms of—

The Admiralty Harbour,

practically enclosing the Roads. Here warships of all kinds can usually be seen, as Portland Harbour and Weymouth Bay together form one of the principal bases of the Atlantic and Home Fleets. The Admiralty Torpedo Works are at the head of the Breakwater.

A path leads from the Nothe by Look Out and the Under-barn to Sandsfoot Castle.

In the opposite direction, below the Nothe, is—

Weymouth Harbour,

its sides lined with shipping, from tiny fishing-boats to the fast steamers for the cross-Channel services. Connected with the harbour is Radipole Lake (*see* below), and between this and the open sea the houses of Weymouth extend from the

53

Pier half-way round the bay. Beyond are the Downs, long rolling stretches of green, for the most part devoid of trees, and looking like a sea with a heavy ground-swell. Here and there are seen patches of chalky outcrop, like white-crested billows breaking on an otherwise uniform green surface.

Radipole Park and Lake

Radipole Lake, the old " Backwater," about three miles long, is formed by the outflow at Radipole of the little river *Wey*, from which Weymouth takes its name. Road traffic crosses by an Embankment Bridge for the rapidly-developed suburb of Westham. The steel viaduct carried the former Portland line, now closed.

The construction of the Embankment and the **Radipole Park Drive,** on the eastern shore, was the greatest public improvement carried out in Weymouth for half a century. It was part of the scheme for the reclamation of the " Backwater," a work that had been talked about in Weymouth almost since King George III began to visit the town.

Previous to the construction of the embankment, the water was half-tidal. Now a pool is maintained at an almost constant level as ornamental water. The Embankment is pierced by eight culverts, four of which are fitted with tidal flaps and the other four with penstocks. In ordinary times the culverts merely take the water brought down by the *Wey*. A notable feature of the Backwater was a Swannery, an offshoot of the famous one at Abbotsbury, and several hundred swans continue to grace the scene. A little crowd of children gathers every day at 10 and 5, thrilled to watch the swan-keeper feed his large family.

The land gained by the exclusion of the sea has been developed as the **Radipole Park Gardens,** with tennis courts and children's paddling pool.

At the upper end of Radipole Lake is a natural bird sanctuary which the Corporation is carefully preserving, and where many rare birds nest.

Statues and Memorials

The King's Statue, erected in 1809 in commemoration of George III's jubilee and "as a memorial to future ages of the virtues of the monarch," stands near the junction of the Esplanade with St. Thomas and St. Mary Streets. On the back of the pedestal is an inscription describing how a number of gentlemen, "being possessed of a statue of his Majesty," presented the same to the town. It has been decorated in correct heraldic colours and the Corporation has laid out a garden to give it a fit setting. The spot serves as a starting-point for the town's local bus services.

The *Jubilee Clock Tower,* in the middle of the Esplanade, was erected in 1887, to celebrate Queen Victoria's Jubilee, and the bronze statue of *Queen Victoria,* near the Greenhill Gardens, was Weymouth's memorial of the Coronation of Edward VII.

The town's *War Memorial* is a plain rectangular stone pillar near the Pier bandstand and Queen Victoria Statue.

A little History

Ralph Allen, of Bath, the original of Fielding's "Squire Allworthy," was the inventor of the bathing-machine. The first was built for him at Weymouth, and he was the first to use it "to bathe his body in the open sea—a treatment so extreme and so strange that it savoured of madness." That was in 1763.

The sun of prosperity shone on Weymouth when George III, after his long illness, took up residence here, and the fame of the new watering-place quickly spread. The most entertaining record of that golden era is to be found in Thomas Hardy's *The Trumpet Major.* Between the years 1789 and 1805, Weymouth was honoured by many royal visits. At Gloucester Lodge, now the *Gloucester Hotel,* George III had long interviews with Pitt, and to the same residence came Lord Loughborough, begging for the Chancellorship, and Addington to ask for the Premiership. Six weeks before the Battle of Trafalgar the King here discussed naval tactics with Nelson's flag-captain, Sir Thomas Hardy, and he penned a daily letter to his son, the Duke of York, then Commander-in-Chief. Gilray, the caricaturist, has left us many interesting cartoons depicting Court life at Weymouth, and Peter Pindar (Dr. John Wolcot) wrote a satirical poem called *Weymouth Amusements,* in which he

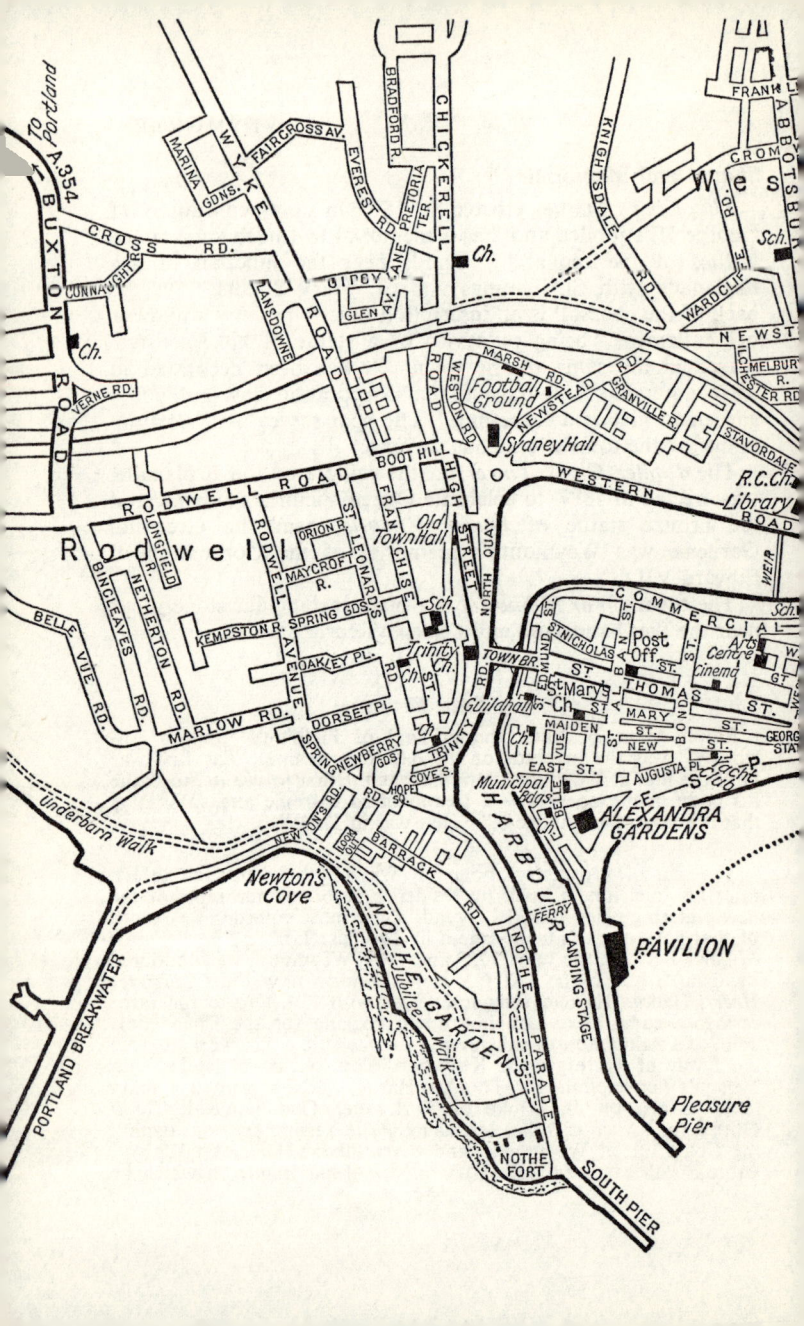

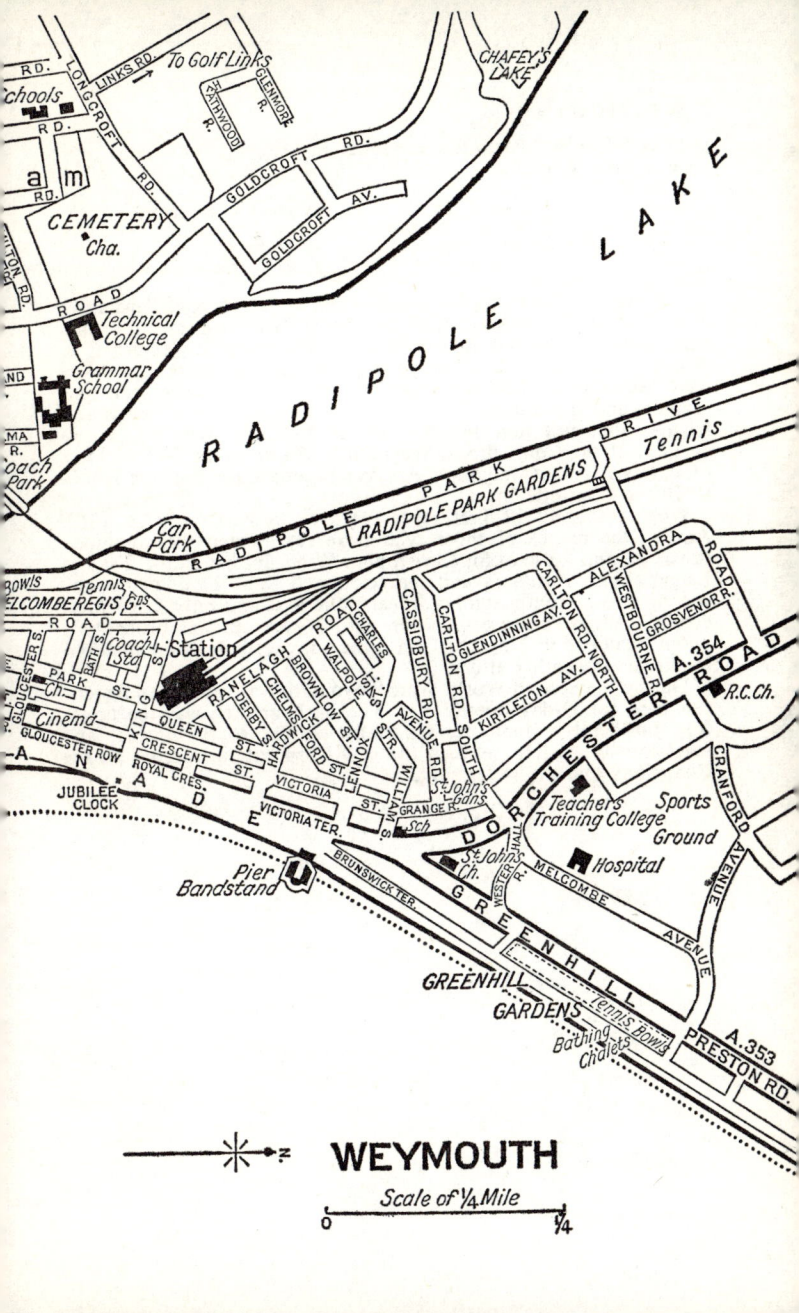

WEYMOUTH

Scale of ¼ Mile

criticized Queen Charlotte's economy in bringing stores and provisions from Windsor:

> " Bread, cheese, salt, catchup, vinegar, and mustard.
> Small beer and bacon, apple pie and custard:
> All, all from Windsor, greets his frugal Grace,
> For Weymouth is a d——d expensive place."

The magnificent man-of-war and a frigate, which rode constantly at anchor for the purpose, took the Royal party on frequent excursions into the Channel, and from these they invariably returned to dinner at four o'clock. The young Princess Charlotte appears to have been a great favourite, especially among the naval officers and seamen, and she frequently went on short cruises in the sloops and frigates that put into the Roads. A full and most interesting account of the Court life at Weymouth will be found in the *Diary* of Fanny Burney (Madame d'Arblay), Second Keeper of the Robes to Queen Charlotte.

Weymouth sent its first representatives to Parliament in 1319. Among the names of those who have represented the combined towns we find those of Sir Christopher Wren, Joseph Hume, Francis Bacon (Lord Verulam), and the celebrated Bubb Doddington, the son of a Weymouth apothecary and the first and only Lord Melcombe. Wren's close association with Weymouth was probably a potent factor in making Portland stone a favourite building material in the seventeenth century.

During the Second World War, Weymouth was used as an American base for D-day operations. The harbour area was the target for considerable bombing, especially on the southern side, and scars are still visible between the new Corporation housing on the Chapelhay and the waterfront.

Walks from Weymouth

Weymouth is particularly fortunate in being surrounded by a wealth of delightful villages and natural beauty spots which can be reached by cliff or country walks. There is no need always to go and return by the same way, as pleasant circular tours may be made, and a bus can generally be used for part of the journey if the total distance is too great.

THE NOTHE, SANDSFOOT CASTLE AND RODWELL

A round of about four miles from the King's Statue.

From the Esplanade cross the Harbour by the ferry near the pier gates and turn to left, along the Nothe Parade. Ascend steps to the little plateau of the Nothe promontory, whence there is a wonderful view. Weymouth Bay lies to the north, Portland Bay to the south, with the grim rock of Portland rising abruptly from the sea.

Portland Harbour is one of the finest in the Commonwealth and is made torpedo-proof by the Bincleaves and Portland Breakwaters, which entirely enclose it on the east, except for narrow ship channels indicated by lighthouses. On the west the sturdy rampart of the Beach is a more complete barrier than any work of man.

Behind the cliffs of Portland, with the old dockyard at their base, may be seen on a clear day the *Verne Citadel* and the chimneys of the Borstal Institution, while in the foreground is a row of huge storage tanks. At the extremity of the Nothe is the Nothe fort.

A walk through the Nothe Gardens leads to **"Look Out,"** a narrow road between high walls at the end of which the beautiful wide prospect comes suddenly into view. "Look Out" may also be reached by the Town Bridge, Trinity Street and Hope Square.

Continuing to the right from the "Look Out," an old

summer house is passed above **Newton's Cove.** This is a converted bathing-machine which tradition claims as the original one used by George III.

After rounding Newton's Cove, **Bincleaves** is reached. An immense amount of stone was taken from the cliff here and used for the Breakwater which runs out from this point. On it are high jetties for testing the torpedoes made in the Admiralty Torpedo Works just to the west. Warning of practice is given by a siren and red flag, and it is most thrilling to watch the long wake of the torpedo and the smoky flare that marks its destination.

The cliff path meets the road leading to the Breakwater. Do not take this, but continue along the cliff by the **Underbarn Walk**—which in common with the Nothe Gardens has been improved and beautified by the Corporation—to **Castle Cove,** a small yacht anchorage with rock pools and sands to offer treasures for children's delight. **Sandsfoot Castle** may be reached by turning to the left along the Old Castle Road.

Sandsfoot Castle

Time and wanton destruction have so despoiled this once fine castle that it retains hardly any interesting features.

It was built in 1539 by Henry VIII, as part of a chain of coastal forts protecting the principal harbours from Deal Roads to Falmouth. Its heavy cannon could cross their fire with those of Portland Castle, just two miles away. Most of its massive structure, including all the gun-emplacements, crumbled into the sea over a century ago, and only the fragment of part of the living quarters remains. Like several of Henry's forts, it was designed only to control the harbour and was very slightly protected on the land side. At a later date a bastioned earthwork, still clearly traceable, was added to give landward protection;

but during the Civil War the Castle never put up resistance. It was maintained as a harbour defence until about 1700, and then allowed to fall into ruin.

Some years ago the Castle and surrounding ground were purchased by the Corporation, which has laid out charming Tudor Gardens and provided for the sale of refreshments.

The return to Weymouth can be made by road through the pleasant suburb of **Rodwell,** through which buses run, or the walk can be extended by a little over a mile by returning through the ancient village of Wyke Regis. For the latter, continue along the coast for a short distance from Sandsfoot Castle to a hollow where there is a passage under the railway leading to the Downclose Estate, where there is a choice of several roads all leading to the main Portland road. This runs straight on to Wyke Church, at which point turn right. At the crest of the hill there are extensive views, including the Fleet and Chesil Bank. The stone marking one mile from Weymouth will soon be reached.

WYKE REGIS, THE FLEET AND CHESIL BEACH

Wyke Regis, little more than a mile south-west of Weymouth, is easily reached on foot or by bus from the King's Statue. The route passes over the Town Bridge and ascends the steep slope of Boot Hill, turning to the right again at the *Rodwell Hotel* to the reservoir at the top of the hill. From here one of the finest views in the district may be obtained on a clear day—Portland to the south, the Ridgeway Hills to the north, and in the west the lovely curve of the Dorset and Devon coast fading away towards Torquay, and the square-topped Golden Cap, a landmark for Lyme Regis, with the county boundary just beyond. In the foreground is the fine tower of Wyke Church, on the hill sloping down to the **Fleet Estuary** and **Chesil Beach,** which run side by side north-westward to Abbotsbury (*see* p. 62).

Off this dangerous ridge many a good ship has gone down with all hands. Indeed, the bay to the west is sometimes called **Deadman's Bay,** on account of the great number of lives lost there. A grave at Wyke contains upwards of two hundred bodies from one wreck. The quiet churchyard also became the last resting-place of nearly a hundred people who were on board the *Abergavenny*, commanded by Captain Wordsworth, the poet's brother, when she was lost in 1805. The vessel struck a corner of the Shambles, although a pilot was on board, and foundered. She carried £70,000 worth of specie and about four

61

hundred passengers. It was from this wreck that a man named Tom-
kins, using a forcing air-pump for the first time, succeeded in recovering
a large sum of money. In 1921 divers found that much of the sand
into which the vessel had sunk had been carried away by the sea, and
they took from the ship two copper bolts which they presented to the
Weymouth Corporation. There is also in the churchyard a tombstone
in memory of a man killed in 1822 in a fight, realistically carved on the
stone, between a revenue cutter and a smuggler—an indication that
smuggling was something more than a little light-hearted evasion of
the law with " brandy for the parson and baccy for the clerk."

Wyke Regis Church, the mother church of Weymouth, is
one of the finest in the district. It was built in 1455 on the
site of an earlier church. The carved heads on the capitals
of the nave pillars are said to represent King Henry VI and
his Queen, Margaret of Anjou. Its tower forms a prominent
land- and sea-mark and commands magnificent views. The
carved coat of arms near the altar was formerly on the tower
of Sandsfoot Castle.

The village lies back from the road and contains many small
Georgian houses. The famous old " Ship Inn " was demolished
by enemy action in 1942.

From the signpost by the church the walk can be continued
on to the **Fleet,** two miles from Weymouth. From the Fleet a
pleasant cliff path leads back to the *Ferry Bridge Hotel* near
the bus stop at Wyke for Weymouth.

The **Fleet** forms a backwater behind Chesil Beach. This sheet of
water, ten miles long, is quite unique. Its greatest width is about
three-quarters of a mile, but in places it is much narrower. Various
schemes have been considered for draining the Fleet, but this is
difficult, since at high tide the sea penetrates to some degree. At the
head of the Fleet, at Abbotsbury, is the famous Swannery of the
Ilchester family (*see* p. 75). The swans regard the Fleet as their
own special highway, for they come and go from Abbotsbury to
the sea at will, and in the mating season build their nests along the
bank.

The Chesil Beach

is the most remarkable and dangerous beach on the South Coast.
The word *chesil* is from a Saxon word meaning shingle. The Beach
is a long, monotonous ridge of pebbles, extending from Portland

to Bridport—about eighteen miles—and connects the peninsula of Portland with the mainland.

It is probably the longest ridge of pebbles in Europe, if we except that of Memel, on the Baltic, above Königsberg. The average height of the Beach is from fifty to sixty feet above sea-level, and its breadth about 200 yards. The raising of this huge natural barrier, which protects Weymouth from the storms of the great West Bay, shows the enormous power of the sea. The pebbles of which the beach is formed consist chiefly of a white calcareous kind, but there are many coloured jaspers and quartz. The greater part have been carried by the storm-waves and tidal currents from the submerged beach near Bridport Harbour, while some have been carried direct to Chesil Beach from the Devon and Dorset coast. Near Portland, where the stones first touch the shore, they are the largest in size and least rounded in form; but as the drift of the currents, and the pressure of the ocean, continually drive them farther and farther in towards the bay, they become smaller and smoother and are so reduced by constant attrition that in a series of years pebbles weighing ten or twelve pounds will become small stones of only a few ounces' weight. The diminution of size is very gradual, and it is said that the local fishermen, when landing upon the beach during foggy weather, can tell their relative position by the size of the pebbles alone. During a storm, the breaking of the waves and the crunching of the pebbles form an imposing sight and sound. The waves mount higher and higher up the ridge, threatening to overtop it, and occasionally they do flood the adjacent lands. On November 23, 1824, a vessel was washed completely over the beach and launched on the Fleet side. The last serious inundation occurred in 1930, when several cottages on Portland Island were flooded to the level of their first-floor windows. When a north wind blows, thousands of tons of pebbles are washed away, to be washed up again when the wind changes. After a storm curious "finds" may be picked up on the beach. The sling stones found at Maiden Castle were brought from the beach.

The stony rampart is a happy hunting-ground for the explorer. The geologist can piece together some of his mosaic of earth history from the pebbles on the beach, the naturalist watch birds and fishes, and the botanist find a rich and varied marine flora.

Warning—The sharp dip of the beach and the terrible undertow render bathing from the ridge extremely dangerous.

RADIPOLE, NOTTINGTON, BROADWEY AND UPWEY

The village of **Radipole**, about two miles from Weymouth, is situated at the northern end of the once navigable Radipole Lake. It has a railway halt, and is on the route of the Weymouth–Upwey buses. It may be reached on foot or by car, either by branching off from the main Dorchester road at the halt—the church lying on the right-hand side of the road about half a mile west of the main road—or by taking the

Abbotsbury road over the Embankment turning to the right at Newstead Road, or by the Radipole Park Drive.

Many Roman remains have been found at Radipole, which is the site of a small Romano-British port.

Radipole Church has an unusual bell-turret with openings for three bells, an exceptional arrangement duly noted in Parker's *Glossary of Architecture*. This church in the old mother church of Melcombe Regis. Near the church is a delightful old Jacobean house, subdivided into cottages, and the scenery at this end of the lake is very charming. The village once boasted a spa and medicinal spring, as readers of Thomas Hardy's *Trumpet Major* may remember.

The new **Church of St. Aldhelm,** in Spa Road, contains several relics from the chapel of the former Weymouth College, a public school founded in the 1860's, which was one of the first casualties of the Second World War. The School buildings now form part of the Training College in Dorchester Road.

Nottington

There is a footpath from near Radipole Church to Nottington, about a mile to the north, or the main Upwey–Dorchester road may be regained through the northern continuation of Radipole Lane, leaving the church left and school right.

Another side-road to the left, Nottington Lane, nearly a mile along the main road, leads in a few hundred yards to **Nottington.** A short way down the leafy road is a curious octagonal **Well House,** built about 1830 and once containing baths and a pump-room. It is now a private house, but is otherwise quite unaltered. Nottington Spa was renowned in the reign of the first George, and in 1719 the celebrated chemist, Godfrey, reported that the Nottington water was the only pure sulphuretted water in England. Near the Well House is a very picturesque old water-mill.

Walkers may reach—

Broadwey,

about three miles from Weymouth, by pleasant field paths from Nottington, while the main Weymouth–Dorchester road passes through it. The little church is built in the Decorated style with Norman doorways and font and Elizabethan oak pulpit. Roman remains have been found in the parish. At

Broadwey the left-hand turning along the valley of the *Wey* leads to—

Upwey,

which lies in a prettily wooded valley. The road passes by the old **Manor House,** dated 1659, and the remains of an excellent Tudor house, now called *Bayard Dairy.* Upwey is part of the old manor of Way Baiouse, named after one of King John's barons, Allen de Baieux. The local name Bayard is probably derived from the same source.

The famous **Wishing Well** will be found at the far end of the village by the church. The well is a natural spring, whose waters were often sampled by George III. The King's gold cup was kept for Royal use at a house near the well, and afterwards was the original gold cup presented by his successors for the Ascot Races. The well is surrounded and completely shaded by trees, forming a delightful dell, in refreshing contrast to the main Dorchester road.

The little **Church** of St. Lawrence close to the well dates from 1267, and is mainly Perpendicular, with beautifully proportioned arches. Among its interesting features are a Saxon font, an internal squint, texts painted on the north wall dating from 1549, and some fourteenth-century Flemish glass in the chancel windows.

A spring whose waters were formerly used as an eye salve flows from Bincombe Clump through the village.

A path leads past the Wishing Well and behind the Church up to the ridge to the south of the village. From here, where the "Cross Dyke" marks the defence or cattle-enclosure of a prehistoric settlement, there is a splendid walk along the hills with wide views over unspoiled country to the sea. After some two miles a break in the ridge gives access to *Corton Farm.* Here in mediaeval times was a hamlet sufficiently large to have its own chapel, and sixty years ago this building was rescued from agricultural uses, restored, and reconsecrated. Services are held there, and the tiny place boasts that great rarity, a mediaeval stone altar, which remoteness or neglect preserved from destruction at the Reformation. From here the walker may continue to Portesham and take a bus back to Weymouth.

Motorists and cyclists who are going on to Dorchester leave Upwey by the road leading up to the main Dorchester road, with its very sharp climb and hairpin bend. Walkers take the old Roman road over the hill and thus avoid the *detour* of the motor road. From the high ground Dorchester is seen in the distance, between three and four miles away, along a perfectly straight road which dates from Roman days. Trees on either side of the road lend shade and picturesqueness to the scene. It is a long gradual descent into **Dorchester.** One and a half miles short of the town, a *detour* to the left opposite the cemetery gates should be made to visit **Maiden Castle,** a hill crowned with ancient earthworks, described on pp. 102-3. The " Castle " is perhaps more pleasantly reached by turning from the main Dorchester road at Broadwey, and taking the picturesque road that leads to the Winterbornes. About half-way to Winterborne Abbas (junction with the main Dorchester–Bridport road) the earthworks are seen on the right. Cars can be taken through the gate to the foot of the slope.

CHICKERELL, LANGTON HERRING, BUCKLAND RIPERS

Chickerell is a village about three miles westward of Weymouth, with which it is linked by a bus service. Leaving the sea-front and passing over the Embankment road the route is through **Westham.** In this case again many people prefer to start their actual walking from Chickerell, and get over the journey there as quickly as possible by bus, for though there are fine views, the road has been considerably built up with houses and factories. The village of Chickerell has a fine church and many thatched cottages, one with mullioned windows dating back to the seventeenth century. The church, said to have been rebuilt in the thirteenth century, has a Norman font, an old priest's door and a Jacobean pulpit. Chickerell lies to the right of the Abbotsbury road.

From Chickerell the less-frequented portion of the **Chesil Beach,** especially East and West Fleet, may be explored. Practically all trace of the old village of Fleet has disappeared. A storm overwhelmed this small place in 1824 and destroyed it except for the chancel of the church and six cottages. Five of the latter were burnt down in 1938. Near the churchyard is an old pound, and about half a mile farther along the road is the later church, built in 1827.

By taking the turn to the left at Langton Cross, nearly two miles beyond Chickerell on the Abbotsbury road, the village of **Langton Herring** will be reached, down a steep hill about a mile from the cross-roads. This takes its name from the old family of Harang or Hering. It is almost concealed by trees, and possesses a small church (St. Peter) with a battlemented tower, Norman arches and a quaint clock.

From Langton a round can be made *viâ* the hamlet of **Rodden** back to the Portesham road, or, for walkers only, along the Fleet to Abbotsbury.

Half a mile beyond Langton Cross on the Abbotsbury road, a road leads east to Nottington, with a little offshoot to **Buckland Ripers,** a hamlet once owned by a family of that name, possessing a fine manor house and a little church, dedicated, as are so many in Dorset, to St. Nicholas. Both church and manor house were burnt down and rebuilt in the seventeenth century.

The round, including Chickerell, Langton Herring, Rodden, Nottington and Dorchester road, where a bus is picked up back to Weymouth, is between nine and ten miles.

PRESTON, SUTTON POYNTZ, THE WHITE HORSE, OSMINGTON AND OSMINGTON MILLS

Buses go all the way to the Mills, the return from which can be made by walking along the cliffs. The road skirts the bay to the east for about two miles, then bears to the left and presently to the right for **Preston.** This is a pretty village, although a good deal of building has taken place within recent years. One of the most interesting antiquities is the Roman tessellated pavement discovered in 1852 and preserved *in situ,* sheltered by a small hut. This is unfortunately not easily accessible. Another is the ancient pack-horse bridge of stone slabs lying to the left of the modern road bridge from Weymouth. Preston ("Priest Town") Church lies just off the main road and is mainly fifteenth century with traces of Norman work.

If instead of turning inland for Preston, the private road along the cliffs is taken, **Bowleaze Cove** is reached. Here are extensive caravan camping grounds and a unique holiday Hotel.

A small road inland between two houses a few hundred yards from the Preston turn ends at a stile beyond which is a field containing the remains of a small *Roman Temple* of the "Romano-Celtic" type common in Britain and Gaul. This consisted of a square "cella" containing the images and cult objects, generally (though not in this case) surrounded by a pillared portico. The site is maintained by the Ministry of Public Buildings and Works (no charge). Only the cella foundations remain but it is worth visiting if only to appreciate how well the site was chosen to be visible for miles in every direction.

Lying half a mile or so to the left of Preston is **Sutton Poyntz,** another typical Dorset village with old thatched cottages near the source of a great part of Weymouth's pure water supply, and interesting as the "Overcombe" of Hardy's novel, *The Trumpet Major.* It is hemmed in by the downs, on which, about a mile to the north-east, is—

The White Horse

with its rider, one of the best known of the white horses to be found in various parts of Southern England. This huge equestrian figure on the hill-side was formed in 1808 by cutting away the grass and earth and exposing the chalky subsoil. It was intended to represent George III and is 280 ft. long and 323 ft. high.

On the Berkshire Downs is the White Horse of Uffington, standing where King Alfred defeated the Danes in 871, and familiar to readers of *Tom Brown's School-days.* Another horse attributed to Alfred is that at Bratton, overlooking Westbury Station, on the Wiltshire Downs. A comparatively modern chalk horse is at Cherwell. It was cut about 1780 and originally had a glass eye made of bottles. In Sussex is the Long Man of Wilmington, and the figure of a giant is cut on the hill at the back of Cerne Abbas (*see* p. 82). Troops camped on Salisbury Plain have at various times carved emblems on the chalk.

A mile beyond Preston, along the hilly main road, is **Osmington,** and a little farther a narrow road leads off seaward to **Osmington Mills.** Crossing the hills, this narrower road gradually descends to the coast, ending abruptly in a group of picturesque cottages, one of which bears the friendly sign, *The Picnic Inn.* A brook that has kept the road company for a little way gurgles round the cottage doorsteps and tumbles into the sea. Osmington Mills is famous for its lobster teas. Beyond Osmington Mills is **Ringstead Bay,** with the fine cliff of **White Nothe,** and the cliff-path passes the site of the vanished village of Ringstead.

UPWEY, BINCOMBE, CHALBURY

This is a delightful walk of anything from seven to ten miles over country between the Upwey and Preston districts described above. There are so many little paths and tracks that distance and direction may be varied indefinitely, and whole days happily spent wandering over the Downs.

Leave the bus at the Royal Oak stop and climb hill by the old Roman road. Crossing the stile on the right, a grass field and the main Dorchester road, follow a by-road opposite to meet the Broadmayne road which has branched at right angles from the Dorchester road. Go along this by the Came Golf Links and woods to a number of tumuli among trees, from which magnificent views over Dorchester and Maiden Castle are obtained. This spot is the famous **Culliford Tree,** which gave its name to a Saxon Hundred. It is now a favourite meeting place for the South Dorset Hunt.

The road turns south to a farm-house something over half a mile away, when a left-hand fork may be taken to **Sutton Poyntz** and **Preston.** A right-hand one passes down Coombe Valley, now largely built up, and skirts the early Iron Age hill-fort of *Chalbury*, with its barrows and hut-circles. It leads to a junction of the Littlemoor and main Preston roads at *Chalbury Lodge* (old people's residence), where bus can be taken, or the walk continued along busy Littlemoor Road to Broadwey.

A visit may be made to the tiny village of **Bincombe,** tucked into a fold of the Downs, by leaving the main Weymouth–Dorchester road at Broadwey (old Station Road) and rejoining it at the famous hair-pin bend on Ridgeway Hill.

The main part of the village clusters near its small Early English church (Norman font).

A century ago, in the days of high farming, the village had twice its present population and was connected by through roads northwards and eastwards, which are now only grassy tracks. With the decline of agriculture after 1824, these roads fell into disuse and left it the remote backwater it is to-day. Most of the old cottages fell into ruin and the school was closed. In the churchyard rest the remains of two soldiers of the King's German Legion, who in 1801 deserted from the camp above

69

the village, took a boat for France, and landed by a fatal error in Guernsey.

A walk over the Downs leads into the Coombe Valley road, and so towards Preston, but it is better to return to the Broadmayne road, so as not to miss the view from Culliford Tree.

BROADMAYNE, WHITCOMBE, WINTERBORNE CAME AND WINTERBORNE HERRINGSTON

A delightful walk or drive of seven to ten miles is to continue past Culliford Tree down the hill to **Broadmayne,** with a plain square-towered church, where turn to the left along the main Dorchester road. About half a mile from Broadmayne there are stone circles in fields on either side of the road just by cottages and a private drive. Another half-mile leads to the tiny thatched hamlet of **Whitcombe.**

The beautiful little thirteenth-century church stands in the midst of ancient earthworks and has a barrel-vault chancel roof, while on the walls are the remains of paintings. It is one of the few Dorset churches to possess original Elizabethan plate. The preservation of the church was carried out in 1912 as a memorial to Rev. William Barnes, who spent two years as curate at Whitcombe. A turning through gates a mile farther on to the left leads into **Came Park.** This is a public road and is remarkable for passing through two beautiful parks—Came and Herringston—before emerging into the Weymouth-Dorchester road. Came Church is near the red-brick Manor House and contains a fine gilded rood screen with linen-fold carvings. **Herringston** is a dignified Tudor manor house. The neighbouring village of **Winterborne Faringdon** is believed to have been completely wiped out by plague several hundred years ago. After leaving Came Park a road to the left by the Golf House leads up by the edge of woods to the Broadmayne road, just opposite the little road to Bincombe mentioned above.

Excursions from Weymouth

I.—PORTESHAM AND ABBOTSBURY

Most people prefer to go straight through to Abbotsbury, leaving the exploration of **Portesham** and its neighbourhood for another time or for the return journey. From Portesham an interesting round over **Blagdon Hill** and past the Hardy monument and the cromlechs can be made either by walking over the heath or motoring along the Portesham–Winterborne St. Martin road to Upwey. A description of this and of Portesham itself is given on pp. 75-6.

Abbotsbury

Road Route (7 miles to Portesham, 9 to Abbotsbury) leaves Weymouth by the bridge over Radipole Lake and runs through Westham, skirting Chickerell and Portesham. It is hilly and narrow in some parts, but the surface is good.

Coaches and Buses several times daily from the King's Statue and Edward Street.
Hotel.—*Ilchester Arms.*
Teas.—*Flower Bowl Café.*

Abbotsbury is situated near the West Fleet, nine miles west of Weymouth. It has two great attractions, a *Swannery* and *Sub-Tropical Gardens.* Other objects of interest, which can be seen at any time, are the *Church* and the *remains of the old Abbey of St. Peter.*

The **Church,** dedicated to St. Nicholas, was rebuilt in the early part of the sixteenth century and is Perpendicular in style, but portions of an older building are incorporated. At its western end is a fine embattled tower containing six bells. Preserved over the west door is a curious figure emblematic of the Trinity. It is that of an old man in a sitting posture, with a crucifix between the knees and a dove at the right ear. This interesting sculpture is very ancient but its date is not known. Against the churchyard wall opposite the north porch are two stone coffins, and in the north porch is a Purbeck marble grave-slab, carved with the figure of one of the early abbots of the monastery, and dating *c.* 1200. This was discovered on the site of the former Abbey Church in March 1788, and placed in its present position at the restoration of the parish church in 1885. An interesting feature of the interior is the pulpit, a fine piece of Jacobean workmanship. It still preserves its sounding-board. Certain holes in the pulpit are pointed out as "shot-marks," and are said to date from the Parliamentary attack of 1644. During the restoration of the roof in 1930 two lead bullets were found in a beam. The seventeenth-century barrel ceiling is of special interest, and bears date 1638 on one of six shields recording Strangeways marriage alliances. The centre panels contain figures of angels. The eighteenth-century altarpiece was given by Mrs. Susannah Strangeways Horner in 1751, and the brass candelabrum in the nave dates from the same period.

On the south side the second window counting from the east has glass from the Abbey. The east window of the south aisle is by Anning Bell, R.A., in memory of the fifth Earl of Ilchester. The registers date from 1567. A list of the vicars from 1312 is preserved in the vestry. An excellent guide has been written by Archdeacon Moule, a former vicar.

The **Manor House,** opposite the church, is a fine sixteenth-century stone building with a beautiful stone staircase removed here from Kingston Russell House.

Adjoining the churchyard is the **Abbey House,** the out-buildings of which include some remains of the old **Abbey of St. Peter.** The monastery was founded in 1026 by Orc, steward of Canute, and was entrusted to Benedictine monks from Cerne Abbey in 1044 (p. 81). All that remains of the abbey church is part of the north wall, which can be seen in the churchyard. Stone coffins and tiles have been excavated near this. To the south-east corner of the church there is a stone building, containing traces of mediaeval work and believed to have been the abbot's house. It is now used as an estate workshop.

To the south lies another fourteenth-century building with Gothic windows, which is known as the malthouse and was probably a kitchen or brewhouse. The gable in the adjoining field may be the remains of the monks' Frater.

To the south of the churchyard is the **Tithe Barn,** or Granary, wherein was stored the grain—the produce of a large neighbouring area. It is 272 ft. long, 31 ft. broad, and dates from the fifteenth century. It is one of the most notable buildings of its kind in the country. Outside the wall, on the south side, are the remnants of the water-wheel formerly used to turn the mill inside the barn. The roof was once covered with the smooth flat stones typical of the county, but thatch has taken their place. The west end of the Granary exhibits good work, but the statuette which once occupied the niche is gone.

St. Catherine's Chapel, now restored, which stands boldly on the summit of a neighbour-ing hill, was built by the Abbotsbury monks in the fourteenth century, and has been described as a perfect mediaeval building of its kind. It is a small but remarkably solid structure, its most interesting feature being the fine stone ceiling  built in the semblance of a timber roof. It was probably intended, like that on St. Aldhelm's Head, as a landmark for mariners and a seaman's chapel. (For a note on St. Catherine herself, *see* p. 79.) A magnificent view in all directions rewards those who climb the height. The easiest path to the summit is approached by taking the first turning on the left beyond the *Ilchester Arms Hotel*.

The Swannery

For the famous Swannery continue to follow the road which leads from the Church to the Barn or Granary. Pedestrians take the shady road which descends sharply on the right. Then walk along a lane, through a gate on the right and across two fields to a large door in a wall. Motorists continue ahead for 400 yds. to the car park (*free*) and take the same route. Close to the door is a board recording that in 1824 the sea was driven over the Chesil Beach and flooded the valley to a depth of over 22 ft. *The Swannery is open from mid April to mid September, 10 a.m. to 4.30 p.m. Sundays from May: admission 2s. (N.B. Dogs not admitted.)*

There are over 500 swans, and several cygnets are hatched yearly. Cygnets take eighteen months before they become fully decked in their white plumage. The Swannery is seen at its best in April and May, when the birds are nesting. A swan lays six eggs each year on the average, of which number five are generally hatched out. It is well to be cautious

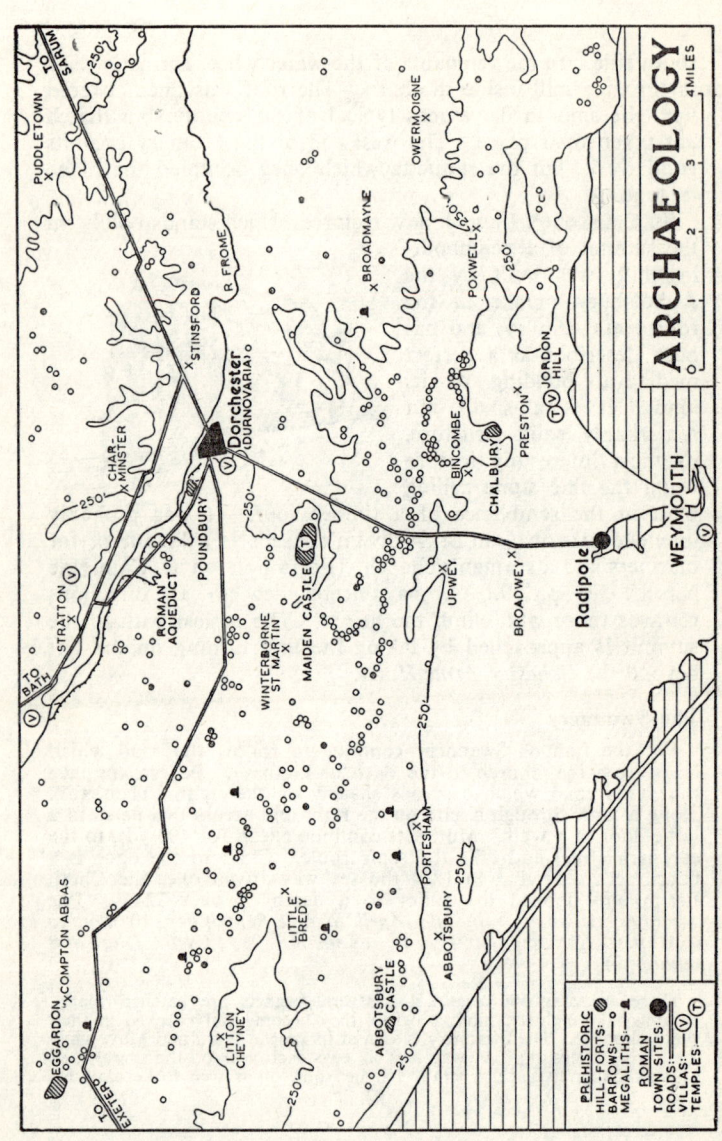

ARCHAEOLOGY

0   1   2   3   4 MILES

TO SARUM

PUDDLETOWN ×

STINSFORD ×

R. FROME

OWERMOIGNE ×

BROADMAYNE ×

POXWELL ×

Dorchester (DURNOVARIA) ○

CHAR-MINSTER ×

POUNDBURY

250'

250'

CHALBURY

JORDON HILL ⓣ

BINCOMBE ×

PRESTON ×

STRATTON ⓥ

TO BATH ⓥ

ROMAN AQUEDUCT

WINTERBORNE ST MARTIN ×

MAIDEN CASTLE ⓣ

UPWEY ×

BROADWAY ×

Radipole ●

WEYMOUTH ⓥ

COMPTON ABBAS ×

BOARDON

TO EXETER

LITTON CHEYNEY

LITTLE BREDY ×

PORTESHAM ×

250'

ABBOTSBURY ×

ABBOTSBURY CASTLE ×

250'

250'

PREHISTORIC:
HILL-FORTS:—◍
BARROWS:—○
MEGALITHS:—▲

ROMAN
TOWN SITES:—●
ROADS:—
VILLAS:—ⓥ
TEMPLES:—ⓣ

Copyright.

when going near a sitting bird ; the swanherd can tell of encounters he has himself experienced when approaching the nest of an angry swan. All day long swans can be seen in the Fleet Estuary (which is brackish water), coming up to the Swannery to drink.

About a hundred yards along the path, within the enclosure to which visitors are admitted, there may be seen on the left a **Decoy,** an elaborate arrangement for decoying wild ducks. Tame birds swim in a central pond, and are joined by wild birds hoping to get food. The former lead the others in the direction of wired-in tunnels, where all species of wild fowl are caught and ringed on behalf of the Natural History Museum.

The Swannery is the private property of Viscountess Galway. Henry VIII granted the Manor to Sir Giles Strangways, Kt., and the grant was confirmed by Queen Elizabeth. It included the swannery, the fishery, water and soil of East Fleet, and the site of the monastery.

The **Sub-Tropical Gardens** are on the opposite side of the village. It is a straight road to them from the church, passing the *Ilchester Arms*, leaving the hill road to Bridport on the right, and taking a left-hand one marked to the *Beach and Gardens*. The entrance is on the left, about 500 yards along the road. There is a free car park. The fine gardens cover many acres, and form one of the most extensive enclosures of the kind in the country, the collection of sub-tropical plants numbering some 7,000 and including beautiful magnolias and camellias. A large number of flowering shrubs are propagated for sale to the public. (*Open, mid April to mid September,* 10 *a.m. to* 4.30 *p.m., Sundays* 2 *to* 6 *p.m., Admission* 2s.)

Abbotsbury Castle, a residence of the Ilchester family, was burnt down in 1913, then rebuilt, but subsequently demolished.

Abbotsbury Castle is also the name that has been given to an Iron Age hill-fort dominating the long, undulating coast road that runs westward *viâ* Swyre to Bridport.

Portesham,

nearly two miles east of Abbotsbury, is one of the prettiest and least spoiled villages in South Dorset. It is cradled in trees, has a cool stream rippling down its main street, and, hilly itself, is dominated by the bare and wind-swept curves of **Blackdown** or **Blagdon Hill,** over 800 ft. in height. The first record of the village is the grant of the manor to Orc by Canute.

The ancient church has relics of many centuries, including a twelfth-century nave wall, a Norman font, a Jacobean pulpit and a well-built tower with an outside turret.

Near the church lies the old manor-house of the village with a Tudor front.

Portesham House is on the south side of the village and at the bottom of the main street. This is a lovely stone house, partly very old, which was the home of Nelson's flag-captain, Thomas Hardy, though he was born at Kingston Russell. The **Hardy Monument,** a tower 74 ft. high, was erected to Admiral Hardy's memory by public subscription in 1844. It is now in the care of the National Trust.

To the Hardy Monument, the way for walkers leads up past the church to the outskirts of the village and then turns to the right through a gateway into a grass field, and onward over the heather to the Monument, nearly two miles away.

Midway between it and the village is **Ridge Hill,** on which is a dolmen called the **Hell Stone.** This was originally the burial chamber of a vanished Neolithic long-barrow. It consists of nine upright stones with a horizontal one 11 ft. long and 2 ft. thick, which were re-erected in the nineteenth century. Near this are other monoliths, and a circle of stones, " the Grey Mare and her colts." In the district are many barrows.

The road from Portesham to Winterborne St. Martin passes just by the memorial, after a very steep ascent from the village, and for motorists improves as it leads round to Upwey.

Anyone who can walk, however, should do so, for the sake of the glorious sense of freedom in the air and the springy turf underfoot and the brooding mystery of the past in the wind-swept barrows and stones.

The road is followed to the right from the Monument to the bottom of the hill, and then a track is taken to the right over the Downs again, keeping to the top of the ridge. Some three miles from the Monument, a long flat-topped mound is reached which is a reservoir belonging to the Portland Waterworks. Here the path turns down to the right to join the Bridport road at Upwey, whence a bus to Weymouth can be taken. (Walking distance about six miles.)

II.—TO BRIDPORT AND WEST BAY

Access.—By bus or coach; by rail, changing at Maiden Newton. Bridport lies about one and a half miles inland from West Bay—there is a frequent bus service between the two places.

Motorists can go by the main Dorchester–Bridport road or the extremely picturesque but sometimes crowded coast route through Abbotsbury, Swyre and Burton Bradstock.

(a) *Route by Main Dorchester–Bridport Road.*

By turning north-westward from Broadwey instead of going right into Dorchester, several miles are saved, the road passing to the left of Ridgeway Hill and Maiden Castle and through three of the numerous Winterbornes, the picturesque *St. Martin, Steepleton,* with one of the two stone spires in the county, and *Abbas,* where is the junction with the Dorchester–Bridport road. All these villages are strung out along a delightful shady road with the silvery Winterborne rippling alongside, ancient trees on its green bank screening the old grey churches.

The road rises out of Winterborne Abbas, passing a stone-circle on the left a mile from the village and a standing stone a mile farther on the right. In fact the whole way along, stones, barrows and earthworks testify to the very ancient occupation of these highlands when the low ground was forest and morass and the people kept to the downs.

The road runs along a ridge, and glorious views are commanded of the smiling fertile Bride Valley on the left, leading up to the high cliff country beyond, and on the right of cultivated and grass uplands.

At **Lee Lane,** a mile east of Bridport, a block of local grey stone commemorates the escape in 1651 of Charles II from capture, in the disguise of a servant.

(b) *Route through Abbotsbury to West Bay.*

A charming though hilly coast road turns up to the right just beyond Abbotsbury village, climbing Abbotsbury Hill, with a gradient of 1 in 7, its sides in July a misty blue with viper's bugloss, and then leads to Swyre, passing within a short distance of **Puncknowle,** which has an ancient little church with a curious font, and a beautiful little Jacobean manor house of exquisite proportions. Inland from Puncknowle lie Litton Cheney and the sequestered villages of the Bride Valley. Below the road, down by the beach, is **Bexington-on-Sea.**

Swyre, a plain little village, is interesting from its connection with the Duke of Bedford (the lord of the manor), whose ancestor, John Russell, was born at Berwick, a farm-house in the parish. Swyre Church, a sixteenth-century building, has some memorials of the Russells. From Swyre the coast road is continued to the picturesque village of **Burton Bradstock**, summer quarters in which are in great demand. There is quite a large colony of artists and handicraft workers. **Burton Freshwater,** where the *Bredy* enters the sea, provides an attractive spot for a bathing picnic. *See* also p. 44.

From Burton the road can be continued either to West Bay or Bridport. A good walk can be obtained by crossing the fields to the beach at Burton Cliff. It may be necessary to ford the stream. Then either continue by the beach beneath the cliffs (here of remarkable interest), or climb to the top and after a mile's walk drop down to West Bay.

For **Bridport,** *see* p. 29.

III.—TO MILTON ABBAS

Access.—Weymouth coaches make the Abbey the object of a half-day trip.

Road Route viâ Dorchester (the town may be by-passed) and then along the main London road, turning left at **Puddletown,** the "Weatherbury" of *Far from the Madding Crowd*. This has an extremely interesting church with a carved ceiling of Spanish chestnut, complete "Laudian" interior furnishings with pulpit, reading desk, and box pews, a sanctuary ring, a rare Gothic chandelier and a curious tumbler-shaped font.

At Milbourn St. Andrew, with a handsome church showing transitional Norman–Early English work, the road turns left to Milton Abbas, nearly four miles away. It runs up a river valley, close to but slightly above the little stream at the bottom, which at every turn shows lovely pictures of farms tucked into little woods.

The road turns sharply to the right at the Park Gates, skirts the lake to the left and then to the right again climbs to the steep village street.

Visitors to the Abbey can leave their cars inside the School entrance.

Milton Abbas stands amidst very lovely scenery. The wooded chalk hills form a semicircle round the picturesque valley and lake enfolding the old Abbey church and the mansion.

The thatched cottages of the village were built by the first Earl of Dorchester, in the middle of the eighteenth century, to replace the old market town which had grown up round the Abbey and which his lordship considered interfered with the privacy of his new family mansion. On the whole it is an interesting example of early planning, consisting of a large church in Gothic style, picturesque almshouses and stoutly built cottages standing in plenty of ground on either side of a very wide street.

Milton Abbey

Milton Abbey, worthy of being named with the magnificent Sherborne Abbey and Wimborne Minster, was founded by Athelstan, the grandson of Alfred the Great, about A.D. 938.  The original building, with Norman additions, was destroyed by lightning in 1309. The present stately structure, still in excellent preservation, was begun in 1322, under Abbot Walter Archer, but was not completed until within a few years of the Dissolution in 1539. The styles range from Early Decorated in the choir to Perpendicular in the central tower (101 ft. high) and the north transept. A "restoration" in 1789 robbed the church of many of its most interesting fittings. In 1865 Sir Gilbert Scott was given the task of repairing the mischief, and he left the Abbey in its present beautiful condition. The lofty reredos is very fine, though the two rows of ornamental niches have been despoiled of the figures of saints that once stood in them. The church has a length of 132 ft. and a breadth of 61 ft., or, including transept, 107 ft. The tower has good details. Some of the painted panels of the old rood-screen, with figures of the apostles, may now be seen in the parish church of Hilton, a mile to the north-west. The old Gothic " Pyx " is absolutely unique.

The mansion incorporates a portion of the former Abbey, the Abbot's hall where a beautiful oak screen bears the date 1498 and the rebus of Abbot Milton. The property is now in use as a school, the hall being open during holidays.

The Abbey Church and St. Catherine's Chapel now belong to the Diocese of Salisbury, the Church being a chapel of ease, and open daily to the public.

On the wooded hill east of the Abbey stands the small **St. Catherine's Chapel,** with thick walls and Norman doorways. After a long period of neglect, it was restored in 1907, so that it could again be used for worship. On the west jamb of the south door is a rare inscription, granting, apparently, an indulgence to those visiting the chapel. As is so often the case, with hill-top churches, the dedication is to St. Catherine of Alexandria, whose body is said to have been buried by angels on Mount Sinai. St. Catherine is the patron saint of spinsters, her day still being celebrated by the " midinettes " of Paris, and the Rev. H. Pentin considered the following rhymes, in use in Milton to-day, may be echoes of mediaeval Latin doggerels:—

"St. Catherine, St. Catherine, O lend me thine aid,
And grant that I never may die an old maid."

"A husband, St. Catherine,
A *good* one, St. Catherine;
But arn-a-one better than
Narn-a-one, St. Catherine."

"Sweet St. Catherine,
A husband, St. Catherine,
Handsome, St. Catherine,
Rich, St. Catherine,
Soon, St. Catherine."

Three miles north-west of Milton Abbas, on the road to Hasel-bury Bryan, is Bulbarrow Hill (902 ft.) with the neighbouring hill-fort of Rawlsbury, from which there are splendid views over the Blackmoor Vale.

IV.—TO CERNE ABBAS AND SHERBORNE

Railway Routes.—For Cerne Abbas there is a choice of three railway stations: *Maiden Newton* (5 miles), *Dorchester* (8 miles), or *Sherborne* (11 miles).
Buses run direct between Dorchester and Sherborne *viâ* Cerne Abbas.

Road Route from Weymouth lies over Ridgway Hill and past Maiden Castle to Dorchester (pp. 93-102). Beyond Dorchester it bears to the left and follows the river *Frome* for a mile. After passing **Wolfeton House** the road bears to the right, where it enters the valley of the Cerne and passes through **Charminster.** From here the road leads to **Godmanstone,** where the *Smith's Arms* is reputed to be the smallest inn in England, and then past **Nether Cerne** to Cerne Abbas (*see* below), which is pleasantly situated among the Dorset downs.

After leaving Cerne the road rises steadily through woodland scenery to *Minterne Magna*, where the parish church contains some interesting memorials to the family of the first Sir Winston Churchill. From here the road continues northward, through scenery immortalized by Thomas Hardy in *The Woodlanders*, to Dog-bury Gate. From the wooded eminence of High Stoy (860 feet), half a mile to the north-west, there is a magnificent view northward over the Blackmoor Vale. On an exceptionally clear day it is possible from this view-point to see the mountains of Wales. After crossing the watershed at Dogbury Gate the road descends from the chalk hills and passes through Lyon's Gate, Middlemarsh, Holnest and Long Burton to Sherborne.

Cerne Abbas,

"Abbot's Cernel" of the Wessex novels, is an exceedingly

interesting and beautiful village, and was once the seat of a flourishing leather industry—gloves, hunting suits and boots were made, and it is understood that the same Cerne family of Hodges who made boots for Queen Victoria also made leather hunting suits for Sir Walter Raleigh. The most picturesque part of the village is the road past the church, which ends abruptly at the fine Abbey House.

Opposite the church is an interesting row of overhung Tudor cottages with outside carving, and at the corner a larger, equally attractive, Georgian house with shell porch. The **Church** has a high tower, ornamented with grotesque gargoyles. A fine Caroline pulpit, with a canopy, bearing the date 1640, and mural paintings of various dates are features of the interior. The medieval rood-screen is of stone. An English oak table, dated 1638, is in the south aisle.

Past the church, on the left, are the old stocks, and just beyond, through the graveyard near the Abbey House, is **St. Augustine's Well,** a shallow pool, very clear, and surrounded with flags and carved stones, while ancient limes and beech trees guard its seclusion. The saint is supposed to have produced the well miraculously by striking his staff into the earth, when water was needed to baptize his newly-made converts. From the spring the water flows through the garden of the Abbey House and flows as a little stream through the village. This is a common and charming characteristic of many Dorset villages.

Cerne Abbey (*contribution box*). The ruins lie beyond the fine Abbey House, now occupied by Pamela, Lady Digby. All that remains of this once powerful monastery is a handsome gateway with very attractive ornamental windows, and a fourteenth-century building a little to the south of it. The latter is reputed to have been a " Pilgrim's house " or " Guest-house ", which for fear of the plague was always built outside the wall.

The Abbey was founded in memory of Edmund the Martyr, King of East Anglia, who met his death at the hands of the Danes, A.D. 870. It was erected just over a hundred years later, in 987, by the Earl of Cornwall, but nothing remains of this first building. Canute plundered the church, but on his conversion restored it. Here Margaret of Anjou sought refuge on the day following her landing at Weymouth, when she received tidings of the defeat of her cause at the battle of Barnet, 1471. The Gate House is orna-

CERNE ABBEY

mented with stone shields carved with many interesting coats-of-arms, including those of the Earls of Cornwall, the founders. The first beacon-light for mariners on Brownsea Island was kept by a monk of Cerne, and the famous Cardinal Morton was a student at Cerne before he entered Balliol.

The first big building seen on entering the village from Dorchester is the Great Barn of the Abbey, now used partly as a residence. The walls are most beautifully made of squared flints in the Norfolk fashion.

Cerne Giant.—Cut in the turf, on the south-west side of a very steep chalk down called Giant Hill (700 feet), and easily seen from the Sherborne road, is the figure of a Giant, 180 feet long, holding a club in his right hand. This figure is of Romano-British work and about 1,300–1,500 years old. It has been renovated recently by the National Trust, to whom it now belongs.

For a description of Sherborne, *see* pp. 106-111.

V.—TO SWANAGE AND CORFE

Routes.—(*a*) By **steamer** to Swanage; (*b*) By **road** *via* Preston, Osmington, Poxwell and Wool, as in the trip to Bindon Abbey (*see* below), and thence through Wareham; (*c*) By rail, a roundabout route *via* Dorchester and Wareham.

Swanage is described on pp. 113-119, Corfe on pp. 140-44.

VI.—TO BINDON ABBEY

Railway Route.—Bindon Abbey is close to *Wool Station*, on the Southern Region line between Dorchester and Wareham. Through tickets are issued from Weymouth.

Road Route: The Abbey is the turning-point in a fine motor excursion from Weymouth. The outward route is usually *via* Preston, Osmington, Poxwell and Wool, where is the " Wellbridge House " of *Tess.* In the first mile or so the road skirts the Bay; then turning inland it passes **Chalbury Camp,** with its barrows and hut-circles, the **White Horse** (*see* p. 68) and, two miles north-east of Osmington, the village of **Poxwell,** which boasts a well with a Gothic stone superstructure, in the manner of the Cornish " Holy Well," a church with a curious round tower and spire, and a most charming old manor house, the " Oxwell Manor " of *The Trumpet Major.* Beyond, at the cross-roads, six and a half miles from Weymouth, is **Warmwell House,** where the gardens are open on certain days.

Owermoigne, Hardy's "Nether Moynton," and once a strong-hold of smuggling, is the next village. The church whose registers make frequent references to the Hardy family for several hundred years, has a tower of great age. From Owermoigne a gradual descent leads to Wool, for Bindon Abbey (*see* p. 147). The return journey may be made southward to the Warmwell cross-roads over Moreton Heath, and, when the rhododendrons there are in bloom, these alone are worth a visit.

Five miles due north of Wool, by a direct road, is **Bere Regis.** The church here has a most remarkable timbered roof presented by Cardinal Morton *c.* 1500, which no-one interested in such things can afford to miss (*see* p. 157).

VII.—TO LULWORTH COVE

Road Route to the Cove may be *viâ* Osmington and Poxwell, turning to the right at the *Red Lion* to **Winfrith Newburgh,** which has a really magnificent church with a fine Norman porch. A narrow road winding between the Downs leads through West Lulworth to the Cove. Coaches take the more circuitous route through Wool and Coombe Keynes.

This delightful little cove is described in detail on pp. 148–150.

VIII.—THROUGH HARDY'S COUNTRY

A motor trip particularly interesting to lovers of Hardy's novels. Further reference is given on pp. 104-5. The route taken by the motor-coaches lies through *Dorchester* (Casterbridge), *Stinsford* (Mellstock), *Bockhampton Norris, Mill Dairy* (Talbot Hays), *Puddleton* (Weatherbury), *Bere Regis* (Kingsbere), *Wool* (Wellbridge), *Poxwell* (Oxwell) and so to *Weymouth* (Budmouth).

IX.—TO WIMBORNE

Road Route as for Bournemouth as far as Bere Regis, then following main road to Wimborne.

Over a thousand years ago Wimborne was a town of repute, the object of many a saintly pilgrimage, the home of kings and the chosen burial-place of one of the most famous of the early Saxon rulers. It is now "a place of deep peace." Its chief feature is its Minster, a structure of great architectural beauty and historical interest. Among much else to be noted within it are an Astronomical Clock constructed by a monk about 1325; the tomb of the eccentric Anthony Etricke, neither in the church nor in the churchyard, according to his vow; and the chained library. The town is fully described in our *Bournemouth Guide.*

X.—TO SHAFTESBURY

Shaftesbury is best reached from Weymouth by road both in going and returning. The route usually taken passes through exceptionally varied scenery, the outward journey being *viâ Sherborne*, past the old chancel of St. Cuthbert and then the glove-making town of Milborne Port, and the return *viâ Blandford* and *Puddletown*.

Shaftesbury is a hill-top town in a magnificent setting. It is one of the ancient and historic Boroughs of the country and now it is as well a market town and fine shopping centre, busy with people and traffic.

In the Town Hall may be seen a number of interesting things, among them the Byzant, an ancient relic of the former dependence of the town for water from the adjoining Manor of Gillingham at the foot of the hill. The Byzant is believed to be unique and has been shown on B.B.C. Television.

Immediately behind the Town Hall is the well known and much pictured Gold Hill with its wall.

At one time Shaftesbury, formerly called Shaston (a name which lingers on the milestones), possessed three mints, a Castle, a Hospital of St. John and eleven parish churches as well as the Abbey and Abbey Church. Of the parish churches St. Peter's in the High Street is the only one which has not disappeared or been rebuilt. It has a massive tower and an ornate parapet along the north side. The western porch is Tudor with fan vaulting.

Of primary importance in the town's history, and the most interesting feature from the point of view of the visitor, are the ruins of the Benedictine Nunnery founded by Alfred the Great in A.D. 888. These are the only remains still extant of any of the great religious houses founded by him.

The Abbey was chiefly noted as a place of pilgrimage to the shrine of Saint Edward, King and Martyr, whose remains were brought there the year after his murder at Corfe, in 979.

The foundations of the Church have now been exposed by excavations, the first in 1861, and the various finds are in a Museum on the site. In 1931 remains were unearthed which may very well be the relics of St. Edward hidden at the time of the Dissolution. They are also to be seen, in the rough lead box in which they were found.

The Abbey Ruins, Park Walk, scheduled as an Ancient Monument, are open to the public from Easter until the end of September; *admission* 2s., children 1s. Weekdays 10–6, Sundays 2–6, or at other times on application at The Lodge.

Portland

Approach from Weymouth.—By road (bus service), passing the old village of Wyke Regis.

Entertainments.—Cinema at Fortune's Well.

Hotels.—*Royal Victoria; Portland Roads; Royal; Clifton; Devenish Arms; Pennsylvania Castle.* There are also numerous inns scattered over the island.

Chief Sights.—Church Ope Cove, Borstal, Rufus Castle, Portland Castle, Chesil Beach, the view from the high ground called Tophil, the Quarries, Pulpit Rock, and the Lighthouse.

Population of the island, about 12,000.

Those who have read *The Well-Beloved* will remember that Hardy, who calls it the Gibraltar of Wessex, says of Portland:

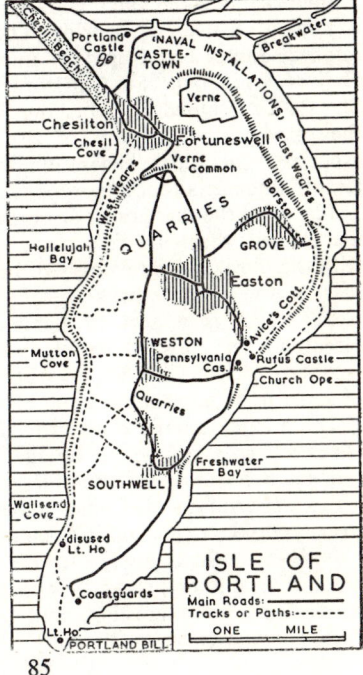

"It stretches out like the head of a bird into the English Channel . . . the towering rock, the houses above houses, one man's doorstep rising above his neighbour's chimney, the gardens hung up by one edge to the sky, the vegetables on apparently vertical planes, the unity of the whole island as a solid and single block of limestone four miles long—for centuries immemorial the home of a curious and almost distinctive people cherishing strange beliefs and singular customs."

"The Isle of Slingers" of Hardy's novels is in reality a peninsula, as the Chesil Bank joins it to the mainland. Portland measures roughly four by

85

one and three-quarter miles, with a circumference of nine miles. It consists practically of one solid mass of rock or freestone, and contains nine or ten villages or hamlets. The names of the villages are purely Anglo-Saxon, and they emphasize the veneration once paid to wells of water. On an isolated rock like this wells of pure water would be an absolute necessity of life, and many of the island villages grew up around a well, as Fortune's Well, Maidenwell, Southwell and Chiswell, the last now corrupted into Chesil. Each of these may be taken as an example of a spring of water influencing the site and determining the name of a village.

The Manor of Portland belongs to the Crown, and the ancient Manorial Court, or Court Leet, with its Reeve and constables, is still summoned annually by Royal Writ.

The island is covered with quarries, and **Portland Stone** is known all over the world. The stone was quarried in the reign of James I and used by Inigo Jones for the Banqueting Hall at Whitehall. Sir Christopher Wren used it in building St. Paul's Cathedral. Fishing and stone-quarrying form the principal occupations of the islanders, many of whom, especially the older generation, represent a curiously dark, almost Phoenician-looking type.

There is little that is soft or tender about the island—outlines are rugged, there are few trees, and in places the eyes ache with the unrelieved greyness—of houses, of rocks, and with the scars of the quarry works.

Yet there is a sort of fierce beauty, intensified by the screaming of gulls overhead and beating of waves on the southern rocks, while the Beach is seldom without the bones of some poor ship rammed and broken on its cruel ridge.

There is a dramatic contrast to this savagery in the sheltered coves where a rich green foliage flourishes, and, wherever it can get a foothold on the cliffs, a wealth of valerian—pink, white and crimson—is found. The Urban Council has planted trees along the roads and in open spaces.

Portland offers many attractions to scientists: fossils, especially ammonites and vegetable remains; curious rock formations; an interesting, though not extensive, flora—one comes across such an anomaly as a palm-tree growing in a perfectly bare street; folk-lore without end for the anthro-pologist.

Its associations with Hardy make it a favourite Mecca for a literary pilgrimage, and "Avice's Cottage" (*see* p. 91) has been converted into a Hardy and Portland Museum.

It is possible to drive over most of the Island from Castle-town to Portland Bill, from Weston to Grove Point. After a visit to Castletown, where one may view the Naval Dock-yard from the battlements of the Castle, a drive to the top of the hill will lead to the magnificent views of Chesil Beach, Portland Harbour, Fortuneswell and, in the distance, the mainland. From this spot, Yeates (*car park*), it is possible to pick a route to tour the Island by car, bus or on foot. It will be noticed on the way into the Island that a wall six feet high and three-quarters of a mile long at the entrance to Chesil screens the railway from the road. It was built for the purpose of preventing the railway engines from alarming horses on the road.

Buses go all the way to Portland Bill, *viâ* Fortuneswell, the bent hill road mentioned below, Easton Square and Southwell. The two—

Breakwaters,

which enclose **Portland Harbour** and render it proof against torpedo attack, are notable works, especially that which was first made. This older Breakwater, starting from Portland, occupied twenty-three years in construction, the first stone being laid in 1849, by the Prince Consort (who went in the first train to Dorchester), and the last stone in 1872. It is in two sections, having a total length of one and a half miles. Between them is a gap intended for the passage of vessels, but owing to the strong currents it cannot be used for that purpose. During the First World War the old battleship *Hood* was sunk across the entrance and is still there. At each end of the Breakwater is a circular fort, with modern armament. The total quantity of stone used would suffice to build a wall 100 ft. high, 40 ft. thick and five miles long.

The New Breakwater begins on the mainland at Bincleaves,

near the Nothe Fort, and extends towards the north arm of the Old Breakwater. It was begun in 1894 and finished in 1903. Its length is rather more than two miles, broken by an entrance gap in the centre. Lighthouses guide vessels through the main entrance to the harbour.

A Tour of the Island

Walkers will probably prefer the cliff walk of approximately eight miles. Leave the bus at the top of the hill at Yeates. Walk across the Common by the side of the Citadel Ditch. Turn right to the Borstal Institute and go through the narrow opening to the cliff path on to the Coastguard Station at Grove Point. Follow the path to Church Ope Cove, where there is a beach café. Leave the cliffs for a short distance for the road to Southwell, where the cliff path goes to the Lighthouse, Bill and Pulpit Rock. From Pulpit Rock there is a good path back along the western cliffs.

Those who prefer to leave the bus at Fortuneswell, instead of going on to Easton, may follow the road northwards to Castletown and the harbour. On the left is the entrance to—

Portland Castle

(**Admission** 6d. Open: April: Weekdays 9.30-5, Sundays 2-5.30 p.m. May to September: Weekdays 9.30-7 p.m., Sundays 2-7 p.m.)

The Castle was built by Henry VIII at the same time as Sandsfoot. Unlike Sandsfoot, when its military value ceased it remained in use as living quarters and has survived in good repair. It is now in the care of the Ministry of Public Building and Works who have restored it as far as possible to its original condition. Anyone interested in the history of fortification would do well to visit it, since it represents a transitional type between the stone castle of the Middle Ages and the bastioned forts of Vauban's period. The plan, which may at first appear confusing, is based on a two-storeyed tower with wings containing quarters, while the casemate for the main battery, originally roofed, occupies the seaward quadrant round the tower. Open gun platforms exist on either side. The grooves in the paving made by the wheels of the gun-trucks may still be seen, and the custodian has a small collection of early cannon and musket-balls unearthed on the site.

From the old village of Chesil, below Fortuneswell, footpaths lead through the West Weares to **Hallelujah Bay**, a

popular place for picnics. Tea and refreshments are available.
The main road from Weymouth, and the bus route, lead to—

Fortuneswell,

a main shopping area. There is practically only one road and
that very much uphill, so the route cannot be missed. The
Public Gardens, with tennis courts and bowling greens, are
passed on the way. On the left is **St. John's Church,** consecrated in 1840. Opposite the Council Offices at the top of
the town the road forks left and right. The left branch leads
to the **Verne,** a site inhabited in prehistoric and Roman times,
where a large dump of sling stones was found.

If this is taken, walk across the Verne Common by the side
of the Citadel Ditch. The fort is now a H.M. Prison Training
Centre. From the corner, heavy guns may be seen on the
East Weares Battery below, and, a little to the right, on
the other side of the road, the low buildings of the Anti-
Submarine School. Far below to the left, and dwarfed by
distance, the old dockyard and harbour look almost like a
picture from the air. Turning to the right, the high wall
surrounding the Borstal Institute (*see* below) is reached, a
narrow gate leading through it along a stone terrace to an
Admiralty Look-out.

The Portland Bill motor road (B 3154) to the right at the
Verne road fork is worth walking up at least once for the
sake of the view to the Isle of Wight, fifty miles away, to
be obtained on a fine day.

The motor road then leads on to Easton. A windowless
structure at a corner on the right is a reservoir. In approaching the town, the prominent tower of St. George's Church will
be seen in the distance towards the right. At the entrance
to Easton a road on the left leads to St. Peter's Church and
to Borstal.

St. Peter's Church was built in 1872 by convict labour. Formerly
the garrison church connected with the Verne Citadel, it now serves
the surrounding district known as **The Grove.** The church has a
good roof fashioned from wood brought from Riga and an altar-
piece in four panels of mosaics representing the Four Evangelists.
The pulpit, font and lectern of Portland stone were carved by Irish

Fenians and Whitechapel thieves, and the fine illumination on wood round the windows was painted by a notorious convict who served three separate sentences under three different names. At the west end of the church is a fine example of a Wheel window.

The mosaic in the chancel and elsewhere was laid by Constance Kent, a fifteen-year-old girl of gentle birth. Penal servitude was her punishment for the murder of her step brother in a fit of jealousy. She was imprisoned in the old Woking gaol, but transferred to a separate part of Portland to carry out the work in the church. A study of her case is given in *Notable Crimes of the Last Century*, and more recently in the book *Saint—with Red Hands?* which reopens the question of the genuineness of her confession.

Borstal

For some sixty or seventy years previous to 1921 the buildings were used as a convict prison. Owing to a progressive decline in the number of law-breakers of the class for whom the prison had been established, the prisoners who were here in 1921 were drafted to other places, and were succeeded by lads and young men from 16 to 21 years of age, sentenced to detention under the Borstal system. The convicts had the opportunity of learning a trade in workshops provided for the purpose within the prison walls, and as such provision is an essential part of the Borstal system, the buildings were admirably adapted for the purpose.

The custodians wear ordinary civilian dress, and are men of culture with a special aptitude for dealing with those in their charge.

It may be said that the Prison made Portland, as the naval construction works were largely carried out by convict labour. The work of development is still in progress, but much of it now is devoted to the improvement of conditions for the boys themselves. One of their achievements is the completion of a stadium near St. Peter's Church. An old quarry has been cleared, levelled and planted with turf brought from waste land in the neighbourhood, making one of the finest sports grounds in the south of England.

At the coast, beyond the school, is a delightful walk of about a mile to **Church Ope Cove** (Ope = opening), which, though somewhat spoilt by quarrying, is a favourite picnic spot, with boats and bathing-huts and pleasant rocky corners.

Extending from Church Ope for more than a mile are the East Weares, a wide tract of undercliff strewn with boulders amid which grow turf, brambles, wild flowers and ferns. The West Weares, of which mention has been made, are on the opposite side of the island.

Motorists who have followed the main road from Fortuneswell and Easton Square should leave their cars at the Public Car Park (*free*) by *Avice's Cottage*, which has been converted into a Hardy and Portland Museum and displays local relics. It is open to the public daily, except Sundays, in summer from 10–5. From October to April on Mondays, Wednesdays, Thursdays and Saturdays, 10–5. The house, built in 1640, and grounds were presented by the late Dr. Marie Stopes.

Above the Cove stands the picturesque ruin of—

Rufus Castle,

sometimes called *Bow and Arrow Castle*. Very little is known of its history, though possibly it was originally built by William II. As it now stands, it appears of late mediaeval date. The stone is native ashlar, hard and durable. The building is now merely a shell, with walls 7 feet thick, and is used as a stable. There were formerly two storeys, the windows being circular. The castle was besieged and captured by Robert, Earl of Gloucester, in 1142, during Matilda's attempt to dethrone Stephen.

Near the castle are some delightful grassy undercliff walks, and adjoining the ruins are the grounds of **Pennsylvania Castle Hotel,** a former mansion almost surrounded by trees, and practically on the edge of the cliffs. The house was built early in the nineteenth century by Wyatt for John Penn, Governor of Portland and a descendant of the historic family. Adjoining the grounds are some few scattered remains of the little Church of St. Andrew, dedicated in 1275 and built on the foundations of an earlier Norman church.

By passing under the bridge at the Cove, and following the road from it, a pleasant Tea Garden is soon reached. Here the road to the left goes to **Southwell,** on the route to Portland Bill, with a right branch to Weston, while the road to the right is followed for **Wakeham,** situated on the main highway, running northward to **Easton.**

Portland's parish church of All Saints is a pleasant building

91

in the Early English style and is constructed entirely of hand-fashioned Portland Stone. The oak pews and choir stalls were the work of Somerset craftsmen.

At Southwell the road from Church Ope meets the one which has crossed the island from north to south through Fortuneswell, St. George's and Weston. **St. Andrew's Church,** locally known as the *Avalanche Church,* was built in 1879 by relatives and friends of the passengers and crews of two vessels, the *Avalanche* and the *Forest,* which were wrecked by collision about twelve miles off the coast.

From Southwell several walks and the road lead past the huge Gunnery School to—

Portland Bill,

one and a half miles, where is situated the tall **Lighthouse.** The most modern in the country, it is usually open to the public on weekday afternoons, between 1 o'clock and an hour before sunset. The light (four-flash every 20 seconds) is electric, has 3,000,000 candle-power, and a range of 18 miles. In foggy weather there is a diaphonous blast of 4 seconds. The old lighthouse, half a mile to the north, was built in 1789. It has now been converted for use as a café.

The headland has developed into a popular pleasure resort with a small beach and some huts and boats. There are guesthouses, cafés and other amenities for visitors (car park).

Of the many rock-tables lying around the headland, the **Pulpit Rock** is perhaps the largest and most curious. There are toe-holes by which the ascent and descent can be made fairly easily. An **Obelisk,** erected by the Brethren of Trinity House, marks the Bill point.

Five and a half miles to the east of Portland Bill is the Shambles Light Vessel, marking the Shambles Sands which extend for four miles east by south of the Bill.

Dorchester

Access.—*Rail* from London, the Midlands and the North by Western Region line and from London also by the Southern Region, as for Weymouth, which is eight miles farther on. There is a quick and frequent service between Weymouth and Dorchester.

Road, from London as for Weymouth *viâ* Salisbury. The road from Weymouth climbs the Ridgeway Hill above Upwey with a steep gradient and acute hairpin bend, after which there is a long straight run into the town over a perfect surface and through an avenue of beautiful trees. An old Roman highway, it is one of the best roads in the neighbourhood.

Banks.—All the five large banks have branches in the business part of the town.

Car Parking Places.—*South Walks Road* (North side) (60 cars); *Fair Field* and adjoining field (unlimited) on market days; *Culliford Road* (West side) and *York Road* (35 cars); *North Square* (5 cars); *Top o' Town* (120 cars); *Charles Street* (70 cars); *Old Market, Charles Street* (100 cars).

Cinema.—Dorchester Plaza.

Distances.—Weymouth, 8 miles; Bridport, 15 miles; Wareham, 17 miles; Bournemouth, 27½ miles.

Early Closing.—Thursday.

Hotels.—*King's Arms*; *Junction*; *Phoenix*; *Antelope*; *Victoria*; *George*; *Sidney Arms*.

Library. — County Library (Central Library and Dorchester Library) at County Hall.

Market.—Wednesday.

Population.—13,500.

Sport.—Bowls and tennis (hard courts) and putting greens in Borough Gardens. Golf at Came Down Golf Club. Hunting with two packs, the South Dorset and the Cattistock. Good cricket club.

At a first sight of Dorchester one at once feels its charm as an old, really English, county town, and the longer it is known, the deeper this impression becomes. It is not perhaps possible to say exactly where the attraction lies, because, though the place is of ancient origin, so many fires, plagues and battles have swept over it that comparatively few ancient buildings remain.

The form of the town has something to do with it—a straight, wide main street, with the beauty that perspective gives to straight lines, rising from the ancient bridges of the Frome on the east to the top of the ridge on the west; a narrower winding street crossing this at right angles and then dropping suddenly to the river; these linked up by intricate little alleys with ancient names; then, girdling the little town, its chief and unique glory, *the Walks*—long shady roads with grass and avenues of ancient trees. These, while so much of the country-side consists of " untameable Ishmaelitish " heathland, as Hardy describes it, and bare whale-backed Downs, make of the sturdy stone town a welcome oasis with a soft green fringe.

Then, as the county centre, it is the old-fashioned mother of a scattered agricultural population in a wide area, and its banks, post office and business premises look large and important, so adding to the impression of quiet busy-ness.

The famous Dorset sheep who browse on the short turf of the Downs and look so wise with short horns curling like spectacles round their eyes, and cattle from the verdant plains of the Frome and Blackmore (Hardy's *Vales of Great and Little Dairies*), are brought weekly to the big cattle market near the stations; there are annual fairs, too, including the great Poundbury Sheep Fair, when ten to twenty thousand sheep are penned for sale.

A market, claimed to be one of the biggest in the West of England, is held each week. Produce of all sorts is brought in, including occasionally the famous Blue Vinney cheese; the travelling shopmen open their stalls for their jolly chaffering; and real old country people gather together from outlying districts, brought by the buses which have ousted the old carriers' vans.

If market-day happens to coincide with Assize Day, Dorchester hums with life. Then, in spite of all modern incongruities, one seems transported to the Middle Ages. The king's representatives—the sheriff of the county and the travelling judge with his suite—the Mayor and Corporation, all in their rich mediaeval robes, meet together and exchange grave courtesies after proceeding to church for the Assize Service. An air of bustle and expectation pervades the town all day, but in the early evening the streets soon become quiet and deserted.

Historical Note

The neighbourhood of Dorchester shows evidence of occupation from early times. The Late Stone (Neolithic) Age is represented by the earthen circle of Maumbury Ring (*see* p. 83), as well as by surface finds of flint tools and weapons. To the Bronze Age belong the Round Barrows which are such a feature of the neighbouring hills, and in the town itself, below the Masonic Hall, was found a burial with the distinctive " beaker " of the early part of this period.

To the Early Iron Age belongs the earthwork of Poundbury (*see* p. 100), to the south-west of the town.

As far as our present knowledge goes, the actual site of the town was unoccupied until Roman times. In accordance with their usual policy, the Roman conquerors laid out and built a new town, as a centre of Roman influence and culture, to supersede the great pre-Roman hill-town of Maiden Castle. Thus arose Durnovaria, situated at the junction of four main roads, close to an easy crossing of the River Frome. The nature of its buildings is testified by the many tessellated pavements found here, and the wealth and culture of its inhabitants by many interesting objects now preserved in the County Museum. An amphitheatre was established in the far older Maumbury Ring; a pure water supply was ensured by an aqueduct or water channel, the line of which can still be traced from its intake seven miles up the Frome.

The town was defended by a town wall, of which fragments may still be seen in West Walks, strengthened, except on the river side, by a triple ditch. There was a cemetery outside the walls at Fordington.

Little was known of the town plan until 1937, when excavations at Colliton Park, within the north-west corner of the Roman walls, disclosed the remains of five buildings. One of these was completely excavated in that year, and proved to be a town house of some importance, with its bathrooms and living rooms, the latter with tessellated pavements. This has been permanently preserved as a historic monument by the County Council, the owners of the site. Recent excavation has revealed further evidence of Roman building.

For over three centuries Durnovaria flourished, with fluctuations of prosperity no doubt, but still a token of the civilization of Rome; but even before the withdrawal of the Roman government it seems that a period of decay had set in. It is unlikely that things improved during the period of anarchy and invasion that followed, but eventually, when the faint rays of history again penetrate the darkness of the Dark Ages, Roman Durnovaria has become Saxon *Dornuuarana ceaster*, whence, by way of *Dorecestre*, its modern name is derived.

King Athelstan, Alfred's grandson, granted it a mint, in common with certain other Dorset towns.

Tradition says that in 1003 Sweyn, King of Denmark, burnt the town and destroyed much of the Roman wall.

The Normans are reputed to have built a Castle on the site now occupied by the prison, and the ruins of the castle are said to have supplied the material for a Franciscan Friary, of which *Friary Mill* (rebuilt), on the bank of the Frome, is a reminder.

During the earlier Norman days the city suffered from the rapacity of the kings, but it gradually recovered its prosperity, and in 1295 sent Burgesses to the first English Parliament. In 1324 two

Bailiffs were elected to take charge of the Borough, a function discharged later by the Mayor and Corporation. Edward III, in whose reign the Black Death ravaged the town, with a consequent trade depression, granted the citizens a charter of perpetual lease for £20 a year. This is still paid annually to the Crown.

The Founder of Massachusetts

Dorchester has many associations with the Puritan emigration to America, the Rev. John White, Rector of St. Peter's Church, having been largely instrumental in planning the colony of Massachusetts.

In 1623 a fishing settlement was established at Gloucester by merchants known as the *Dorchester Adventurers*, and, though it did not prove a success, some of the settlers remained in the country, at Salem.

To take possession of a grant of land given to them and other settlers, now known as the New England Company, *John Endicott* of Dorchester and fifty others went to Salem, and later the New England Company was given a charter calling it the self-governing colony of Massachusetts. The colonists who went from Dorchester and the surrounding districts were instructed by the Rev. John White, who accompanied them to Plymouth, and formed them into a Church Society, to build a church as soon as they landed from the " Mary and John." This they did, and called it the *Daughter of John White*, at Dorchester, Massachusetts, which held its tercentenary in 1930, prominent citizens from Dorchester, England, attending the celebrations.

In the Civil War of the seventeenth century, Dorchester sided with the Parliament. After making but a show of resistance it was in 1642 temporarily occupied by a Royalist force, members of which sacked the house of the Rector of Holy Trinity and of St. Peter.

Later, in 1644, the Earl of Essex took possession of the town for Parliament, and in 1645 Cromwell paid a visit.

Here, too, Judge Jeffreys held his " Bloody Assize " in 1685 after Monmouth's rebellion. An oak-panelled room in the *Antelope Hotel* is said to have been the scene of the trials, described vividly by Macaulay. It will be recalled that 312 prisoners were then tried for treasonable sedition, and that all but twenty received sentence of death in a batch, having been led to plead guilty by the pretence that only thereby was there any chance of saving their lives. About three of every four did indeed escape capital punishment, about eighty being hanged, drawn and quartered.

The house in which Jeffreys lodged is in the High West Street (*see* p. 98), but Dorchester has comparatively few other old buildings, mainly because it has been the prey of four great fires. On August 6, 1613, there broke out a fire which destroyed three hundred houses. In January, 1622, thirty-five houses were burnt down; three years later fifty-seven were consumed, and exactly fifty years after that catastrophe forty houses fell in a fire that would probably have destroyed the whole town, but for the exertions of a regiment of dragoons, quartered at Dorchester.

In 1834, George Loveless and other farm labourers were tried in the Shire Hall and received sentences of transportation. Known as the "Tolpuddle Martyrs," their story figures in the history of the Trade Unions. The Old Crown Court, where the trial took place, is no longer used since the opening of the new County Hall. It was purchased by the Trades Union Congress as a memorial and is open to the public, on application to the adjoining R.D.C. offices. Mon.–Fri. 10.30–12.30 and 2–4.30. At other times by arrangement.

Everyone interested in the Trades Union movement in this country should visit its birthplace at Tolpuddle, about six miles to the north-east of Dorchester. There are various memorials to the pioneers, including an arch in front of the Methodist Church, unveiled by the late Mr. Arthur Henderson in 1912, and six picturesque thatched cottages with the following dedication in front: "These cottages were erected by T.U.C. as a memorial to the Tolpuddle Martyrs and may be inspected at the George Loveless cottage." There is also a tablet on the cottage occupied by Thomas Standfield, one of the pioneers.

The Town

Dorchester is built on high ground west of the spur of land between the Frome and its tributary, the Winterborne.

Into the town enters on the east, by bridges over the Frome, the London road, following an old Roman highway. It continues through the town as High East and then High West Street, emerging at the former Depot Barracks and going on to Bridport.

From the south-west the tree-planted Weymouth Road, also a Roman highway, runs into the town on the south, passes up as the narrow South Street, crosses the High Streets at a typical "Carfax," and then continues as North Square—which is not really a square at all, but a rather wide street, formerly known as "The Bull Stake." This narrows suddenly, and, with other parallel little alleys, continues as Friary Lane down to the river.

High East Street is a wide straight street rising gradually from the Frome. A turn to the left immediately after crossing the river leads up Fordington Hill to St. George's Church.

The church on the left of the street with a high spire is *All Saints,* rebuilt in 1845. In 1662 its rector was ejected for nonconformity and founded an Independent church, now represented by the Congregational Church. The church contains a good Jacobean pulpit.

At the cross-roads the **Town Hall,** an ornate modern building, Tudor in style, occupies one north corner, while the opposite one is nobly filled by *St. Peter's Church* (*see* below).

From the cross-roads the main street continues up the hill as **High West Street,** with St. Peter's Church, the *County Museum* (*see* below), *Holy Trinity Church,* several times rebuilt, the last in 1875, the Shire Hall, and some quaint old houses on the north side. With its back to the houses at the corner and facing along the Bridport Road is the **Hardy Memorial,** a bronze sitting figure with a stone base, the work of Eric Kennington.

Close to the Memorial is the entrance to **Colliton Park,** where in 1937 a **Roman House** was completely uncovered (*see* p. 95) and is now preserved permanently as a historic monument. **County Hall** and **Crown Court** are in the park.

On the south side of High West Street the most interesting building is the large and picturesque Tudor House commonly called **Judge Jeffreys' Lodgings,** from the tradition that it was occupied by the notorious Lord Chief Justice in 1685, when he held the Assize at which he covered his name with infamy. Now in use as a restaurant, it has retained its little gallery, the greater part of its woodwork and several stone-mullioned windows.

A little farther up the road is the *Roman Catholic Church* of Our Lady Queen of Martyrs and St. Michael. It is in the Early English style, the materials being those of the Church of St. Michael, Westport, Wareham. The road to Bridport passes on its right the imposing Keep of the former Depot of the Dorset Regiment, which now houses the **Dorset Military Museum** (1s., 9–5), with its collections of the Devonshire and Dorset Regiment, Militia, Volunteers and Queen's Own Dorset Yeomanry. The museum covers two floors and incorporates a well stocked reference library of military works. About five minutes' walk from the keep the masts of the **Post Office Radio Station** come into sight, prominent for many miles around. The masts are 287 ft. high, and each aerial covers an area of nearly 3 acres. The station is in direct communication by land-line with the London overseas telegraph headquarters, and operates direct radio telegraph and picture services with many parts of the world.

South Street is the continuation of the Weymouth Road through the town to the cross-roads. Opposite the chief **Post Office,** with a War Memorial tablet designed by Thomas Hardy, are **Napier's Almshouses.** The inscription above reads "Napier's Mite, 1616." The building was erected in that year by Sir Robert Napier, or Napper, ancestor of Lord Alington, the present patron. Picturesque portions are the cloister, adjacent to the street, and the guest chamber, called the Xenodochium. The little court or quadrangle is practically as it was three hundred years ago, though the old people were moved elsewhere some years ago. When this happened the building was threatened with demolition but it has been thoroughly and delightfully restored and is now used as business premises. The clock came from the old Work-house.

The modern store adjoining occupies the site of the old grammar school founded in 1569 by Thomas Hardye.

At the High Street end is the **Cornhill,** where stands an obelisk called the **Town Pump,** erected in 1784 to mark the site of an ancient cupola which had become ruinous.

The river can be reached by leaving the *Prison* (on the site of the ancient castle) on the left, and descending the steep **Friary Hill.** Turn to the left and follow the stream along till, turning a corner to the left again, *Hangman's Cottage,* a picturesque thatched building, is seen.

The square can be completed by ascending Glyde Path Road to High West Street, following the fine old wall of *Colliton House.*

The Walks

These are beautiful avenues of limes, chestnuts and sycamores which surround the town on three sides and follow the lines of the old Roman Walls, which enclosed eighty acres. **Bowling Alley Walk,** to the west of the Weymouth Road, **West Walk,** continuing from that to High West Street, and **Colliton Walks,** from High West Street downhill by the side of Colliton Park, were planted between 1702 and 1723. The only remnant of the ancient stone wall forms part of the garden boundary wall of the house at the top of High West Street, at the upper end of the Borough Gardens. It is indicated by a tablet.

South Walks, east of Weymouth Road, and **Salisbury Walk,** on the east side of the town, were planted about 1743. In addition the Weymouth and Bridport Roads were planted with trees about the end of the eighteenth century.

A short distance along the Weymouth road is **Maumbury Ring,** a rampart, circular in plan, with an entrance at the northern end. The astonishing history of this work was revealed by excavation (1908-13). It dates back to Late Neolithic-Early Bronze Age (*c.* 1800 B.C.), when it was built as a sacred circle with a ditch inside the rampart. The ditch had silted up by Roman times, when it became the amphitheatre of Roman Dorchester. In the Civil War it was converted into a redoubt for defence against attack by the Royalists from Weymouth. In the eighteenth century it was used for public executions and it is still frequently used for the less barbarous public meetings of the present day.

Poundbury, or **Pummery,** is an Early Iron Age fort half a mile north-west of the town. Both this earthwork and Maumbury Ring were nearly destroyed in the early days of railways, and it was only after personal appeals to Brunel that in the latter case the railway was slightly diverted, and in the former a tunnel was made beneath it. Poundbury is of Early Iron Age date, as proved by excavations carried out during the year 1938.

St. Peter's Church

is a venerable building of very ancient origin. The present church is nearly all fifteenth-century work.

Tradition says that it was erected by " Geoffrey Van, his wife Ann, and his maid Nan."

The building is referred to in Hardy's novel, *The Mayor of Casterbridge,* as " a grizzled church whose massive square tower rose unbroken into the darkening sky." The tower, 90 ft. high, contains a peal of eight bells of beautiful tone.

Against the tower is a bronze *Statue of William Barnes,* poet, philologist, antiquary, and rector, from 1862 to 1886, of Winter-borne Came (one of more than a dozen places called Winterborne), a small village, two miles south-east of Dorchester. His learning, his writings and poems in the Dorset dialect, his kindliness to his poor and his parish, made Barnes universally beloved. The pedestal bears the simple inscription—" William Barnes, 1801 to 1886," and the following lines from his poem, *Culver Dell and the Squire*—

> " Zoo now I hope his kindly feäce
> Is gone to vind a better pleäce ;
> But still wi' vo'k a-left behind,
> He'll always be a-kept in mind."

The arch of the inner doorway of the neighbouring **South Porch** is Transitional in style. It is Pointed, but Norman detail is used. It was in an older church of St. Peter, and was built anew, stone for stone, in the fifteenth century.

The interior of the church is worth careful inspection. The tower is supported by a lofty arch. At the west end of the north aisle is a monument to the memory of *Denzil, Lord Holles*, who distinguished himself in the Long Parliament. An inscription records his virtues. Below is a glass case containing a copy of the Breeches Bible, 1594, and a copy of the *Troubles of Jerusalem's Restauration*, 1645, by John White.

It will be remembered that he was one of the two Members who held the Speaker in the chair while Sir John Eliot read his remonstrance addressed to the King against the levying of the tax known as Tonnage and Poundage, and later one of the five members accused by Charles I of high treason, whom the King went personally to the House of Commons to arrest. After the Restoration Denzil Holles was raised to the peerage.

Another interesting memorial recalls the fact that the family of Thomas Hardy has been for centuries associated with the district which he immortalized. The memorial is to a Thomas Hardy who in 1569 founded the Dorchester Grammar School, " endowing this Boroughe," as the inscription records, " with a yearely revenew of 50 L; a schoolmaster, 20 L; an usher, 20 nobles, and almswomen, five marks. The Baylives and Burgisses of Dorchester, in testimony of their gratitude, and to commemorate to posterity an example so worthie of imitation, have erected this monument." The east end of the south aisle has been panelled with fine old oak, and set aside as a *Hardy Memorial Chapel*.

In the north pier of the chancel arch opening into the north aisle are remains of the stairs to the rood loft. They have been adapted to form the approach to the **Pulpit,** a good specimen of Early Jacobean work.

The carved **Reredos,** depicting the Last Supper, is an excellent piece of modern workmanship, very beautifully shown up by flood lighting. In the south-east corner of the church are two cross-legged effigies, which came from the Priory church. They are usually called the " Crusaders," but belong to the period of the final stage of the transition from mail to plate, 1360 to 1405, and therefore they are at least a century later than the last crusade of 1270.

The County Museum

(Admission charge. Open 10 a.m. to 1 p.m. and 2 p.m. to 5 p.m. on weekdays.)

Adjoining the church is the Dorset County Museum, owned and administered by the Dorset Natural History and Archaeological Society. Its collections are chiefly concerned with the Geology, Natural History, Prehistory and History of Dorset.

In 1952 the Thomas Hardy Memorial Room, with its reconstruction of Thomas Hardy's study at Max Gate and original manuscripts of his poems and novels, was considerably enlarged to house the growing collection of Hardiana, now unequalled in Europe. Recent accessions include the extensive E. N. Sanders Library of publications of Hardy's works and books on Hardy's life and achievements. Near by are shown relics of other Dorset Worthies, notably the Rev. William Barnes (*see* reference on page 100).

The Natural History Galleries, also opened in 1952, have since been enriched by the acquisition of the C. Holland Warne Collection of Birds, the C. D. Day Collection of Dorset Insects and the A. G. B. Russell Collection of Lepidoptera.

On the first floor is the Geology Room, with geological relief models of Dorset and a comprehensive collection of fossils.

On the ground floor of the Main Hall are the archaeological collections resulting from nearly two hundred years of excavation and collecting in the county. The museum is particularly rich in prehistoric and Roman material.

In the gallery of the Main Hall objects dating from the Saxon period to the present day are exhibited: these include eighteenth and nineteenth-century costumes and uniforms.

The Museum Library (extra charge for non-members) has a special section of Dorset books and papers.

Maiden Castle

The finest of the Dorchester earthworks and one unsurpassed in this country for the magnitude and complexity of its defences is **Maiden Castle**, just under 2 miles to the south-west of Dorchester. To reach it follow the Weymouth road past Maumbury Ring and turn to the right opposite Dorchester Cemetery. For the following notes we are indebted to the courtesy of Sir Mortimer Wheeler, who has directed important excavations.

The name is one which occurs in various forms throughout Europe and as far east as Syria, but its interpretation is uncertain. In its present form, Maiden Castle dates from the first century B.C., but excavation has shown that under the eastern part of it lies a Neolithic town or village of about 2000 B.C., outlined by two rings of entrenchment no longer visible on the surface. After the abandonment of this village, but still within the Neolithic period, an immense mound 60 ft. wide and 1,740 ft. long was built along the ridge. This remarkable mound is no longer visible on the surface, but its eastern end, within which was discovered a muti-lated human skeleton, lies buried just south of the visible foundations of the Roman temple. After about 1500 B.C. the hill-top was deserted until the latter part of the fourth century B.C., when the earliest portion of the existing earthworks was built on the site of the Neolithic settle-ment by people whose ancestors had, in part at least, come from Northern France and had settled widely over Southern England. The builders used tools of iron, grew wheat upon the surrounding slopes and lived in timber hutments within the enclosing earthwork. Subsequently, the population grew in numbers and the enclosure was extended, possibly about 200 B.C., to its present western limit.

Later in the first century B.C., the ramparts were enlarged and most of the outer defences were added under the direction of invaders who came from Brittany and mastered a great part of south-western Britain. A stone parapet, now destroyed, was built round the main rampart and the entrances were lined with massive stone walls of which traces, recently excavated, can be seen at the eastern end. At this time Maiden Castle was in its prime; its population may have amounted to some 4,000 or 5,000 persons, who lived in crowded timber huts often equipped with storage-pits cut deeply into the chalk. In addition to tilling the sur-rounding lands, these people kept large flocks of sheep and herds of cattle, and had dogs of about the size of a modern foxhound. Their clothing was woven with the aid of looms equipped with loom-weights of chalk and clay.

At the time of the Roman invasion of A.D. 43 the eastern entrance was stormed by Roman troops, and in 1937 the "war-cemetery" of the defenders who fell with sword- or arrow-wounds in the fighting was found just outside it. After the capture of the town, the defences were par-tially dismantled, but occupation of the site continued for some twenty years longer.

Finally, some three centuries later, the Romano-British inhabitants of the neighbourhood built a temple and at least two other small Roman buildings on the eastern hill-top within the prehistoric defences. Votive objects found in the temple (the foundations of which are still visible to the public) include a small bronze Celtic bull, the emblem perhaps of a Water Deity. At some date subsequent to the Roman occupation—perhaps in the fifth century A.D.—the hill-top was finally deserted, save for occasional visitation by bands of Saxons, one of whom was buried with his scramasax near the remains of the temple. Since that time the Castle has remained, in the words of Thomas Hardy, a "stupendous ruin," sprawling across the downs.

Fordington St. George

is on the east side of the town. The church, the first to be dedicated to St. George in England, retains portions of the original Saxon and Norman structure, the principal being a tympanum having a finely preserved representation of the patron saint aiding the crusaders and discomfiting the Saracens, during the siege of Antioch. The stone pulpit is inscribed 1592. The tower, 80 ft. high, is decorated with delicate tracery; it dates from the fifteenth century, when considerable additions were made to the church. Two of the six bells are pre-Reformation.

Standing against the tower arch is a Roman inscribed grave slab found in 1908 during an enlargement of the church, the Normans apparently having used it as a support for their new tympanum. It is first-century and bears the inscription, " To Carinus, a Roman Citizen, aged 50 years, Rufinus and Carina and Avea his children, by Romana his wife." In the north aisle is a medieval stone altar from Salisbury Cathedral.

Ten miles west of Dorchester, along the old Roman road to Exeter, lies the Iron Age hill-fort of **Eggardon,** contemporary with Maiden Castle, 800 ft. high. Splendid views from this point, to West Bay and across the Vales, make the trip worth while even to those not so interested in prehistoric earthworks. Four miles out of Dorchester the Roman road carries straight on when the modern Bridport road bears left, and from this point it runs in a series of straight sections along the ridge. It is narrow, but the surface is fairly good and quite easy for cars. The road may be followed all the way to the *camp*.

A Hardy Pilgrimage

So close was the connection between Thomas Hardy and the corner of the country where his ancestors had lived for generations and which he himself loved so well, that it is possible, in a short walk of two or three miles, to see his birthplace, school, home, and the spot in old Stinsford Church where his heart is buried.

Thomas Hardy was born on June 2, 1840, in an old house in the hamlet of Higher Bockhampton, on the edge of the wild and primitive moorland he called " Egdon Heath." He went to the little village school at Lower Bockhampton (the " Melstock " of *Under the Greenwood Tree*). His father was a builder, and he himself, intending to become an architect, was articled in Dorchester and later removed to London. His literary genius, however, would not be denied, and he published his first book, *Desperate Remedies*, in 1871. Many novels and poems followed: *The Dynasts*, an epic, the finest of the latter, and *Tess*, probably the best known of the former.

Hardy built himself a secluded house, Max Gate, just off the Wareham road about a mile from Dorchester. He died there on January 11, 1928.

To make the pilgrimage of the " shrines," it is perhaps better to walk, as there are some footpaths which may be taken. It is quite possible to go by car (however unorthodox a pilgrimage), although the side roads are narrow.

First go along the Wareham road out of Dorchester, passing on the left, nearly a mile from the town, *Max Gate* at the corner of a side road leading to the left. Keep straight on along the main road for about 200 yards, and then take the left fork. This crosses the railway after about half a mile, and then, bearing round to the left (leaving the West Stafford road on the right), descends into the green "Vale of Great Dairies," where the Frome, with countless little daughter channels, meanders through its wide flood-plain.

Lower Bockhampton is a long grey village, where Hardy's little school (now private residence) may be seen, on the hilly road just beyond the river. The Greenwood Tree was considered unsafe and cut down. At King George V's Silver Jubilee another was planted and rails were put round to protect it.

Continue straight up through the village, past cross-roads with a signpost pointing to Tincleton on the right and Dorchester on the left, till a small road is reached leading off to the right at a post box. Go along this between farm buildings until a tiny hamlet, **Higher Bockhampton,** is reached. At the very end of this, and on the edge of **Puddletown Heath** (Hardy's "Egdon"), is an old thatched house with crossbeams and lattice windows, his birthplace. Opposite it and on the edge of the wild moor country is a granite obelisk, "Erected by a few American admirers in 1931."

To get to Stinsford, either return to the cross-roads mentioned above and turn to the right, reaching the church in about a mile, or else take a footpath nearly opposite the little Higher Bockhampton road through *Kingston Park* (the "Knapwater House" of the Wessex novels). This leads on to the **Stinsford** ("Mellstock") road. The church, dedicated to St. Michael, lies back a little from the road, but a side road leads to it and cars may be turned round a tiny green.

It is a little quiet grey building with plain tower and grotesque gargoyles. Inside there is a window on the south erected by public subscription, and also an organ presented by Miss Hardy in memory of her parents, brothers and sister. Oak panelling from Kingston Manor lines part of the Church, and another point of interest is the Norman font, restored in 1920. In the churchyard, shadowed by an old yew-tree, Hardy's heart—his ashes lie in Westminster Abbey —is buried beside the grave of his first wife and close to generations of his ancestors.

Stinsford may also be reached from Lower Bockhampton by a gravel path near the bridge.

The round may be extended to **West Stafford,** where Tess and Angel Clare were married in the little church.

Sherborne

Buses.—Between Yeovil (5¼ miles), Sherborne, Salisbury, Stalbridge, Shaftesbury and Dorchester.

Churches and Chapels.—*Abbey Church of St. Mary the Virgin*; *St. Mary Magdalen*, Castleton; *St. Paul's*, McCreery Road; *Roman Catholic*, Westbury; *Methodist*, Cheap Street; *Congregational*, Long Street; *Baptist*, North Road.

Early Closing.—Wednesday.

Fishing.—Coarse fishing may be obtained in the neighbourhood.

Golf.—There is an 18-hole course 2 miles from the town.

Hotels.—*Half Moon*; *Antelope*; *Saffron*; *Crown*; *Plume of Feathers*; *Swan*; *Eastbury*; *Black Horse*.

Hunting.—Sherborne is the centre of the Blackmore Vale district and is within easy reach of several other hunts.

Population.—7,730.

Post Office.—Cheap Street.

Road Excursions.—To Dorchester, Weymouth, Bridport, West Bay, Lyme Regis, Bournemouth, Torquay, Glastonbury, Wells, Cheddar Caves, etc.

Sherborne is an ancient warm-tinted stone town set like a gem among green hills on the northern border of the county, and on the banks of the " Clear Stream " or Scir Burn which gives it its name.

It is famous for its Abbey Church (founded as a Cathedral) and its School. Other interesting structures are its Almshouses, Castle, Conduit and many old houses. The centre of an agricultural and pastoral district, Sherborne's industries include glove factories, silk mills and creameries.

Historical Note

The history of the town is largely the history of the Abbey, until the Civil War, when strife centred round the Castle.

In its earliest days the kingdom of Wessex had but one bishop, whose seat was at Winchester, the capital of the kingdom. At the close of the seventh century it was decided to divide the unwieldy diocese and to establish a separate see at Sherborne, or *Scir-burn* (" clear brook "), as the name was then written. The first bishop, St. Aldhelm, as we call him, was consecrated in 705, and was the builder of the original Cathedral. About the same time the School was founded. There is a tradition that within it Alfred the Great received his early education. In 1075 the See was moved to Old Sarum, but the attached monastery continued at Sherborne.

In the early days of the town the monks allowed the townsfolk to use the western part of the nave of the Abbey Church as a Parish Church.

106

In the fourteenth century Allhallows Church was erected for the parishioners. It was built on to the west end of the Abbey Church. It had not the status of a parish church, and therefore Sherborne children had still to be baptized at the old font. This came to be regarded as a grievance, which was aggravated by the monks removing the font to what the townsfolk alleged was a less convenient site. To get to the font the townsfolk had to enter their own church and to pass from that through the doorway to which attention is directed later. The monks had partly closed the original opening and constructed the existing smaller doorway, " inconveniently small," said the townsfolk, who finally set up a font in Allhallows. This the monks regarded as an infringement of their rights. They also complained that the bells of Allhallows rang for matins at far too early an hour, and disturbed their slumbers. The dispute was referred to the Bishop, who ordered both parties to make concessions, a judgment that gave satisfaction to neither.

The townsmen rose in " playne sedition," in 1437, and a priest of All-hallows shot into the Abbey Church a flaming arrow which set on fire the roof, and damage to the sacred buildings resulted. Traces of the fire are clearly seen in the dark red on the stones of the nave and choir. The monks gave way to the wishes of the parishioners, and rebuilt and restored the choir, compelling the now conscience-stricken townspeople to con-tribute to the expense. The famous Pack Monday Fair is held annually on the first Monday after October 10.

The monastery was dissolved by Henry VIII, and the monks dispersed. Since its purchase this magnificent building has continued as the Parish Church of Sherborne.

The Abbey Church (St. Mary the Virgin)

Open to inspection all day. There is a box for voluntary contributions. The only fixed fee is for admission to the tower, 6d. As far as possible visitors will be conducted round the Abbey if they so desire.

Dimensions.—Length, 230 ft.; height of tower, 109 ft.; width of nave and aisles, 61 ft.

By reason of its matchless interior and interesting history this fine old building commands first attention. It is chiefly of Perpendicular architecture, but the tower and transepts exhibit their Norman origin. The porch by which visitors enter, at the west end of the south side, is also Norman. In the nave the eye is at once attracted by the magnificent fan vaulting of the roof, only surpassed by that of the choir. It is the work of Abbot Ramsam, who restored the nave and gave it its beautiful Perpendicular windows (1475–1504). The bosses are interesting by reason of their variety. The designs include the initials of Henry VII and Elizabeth of York joined by a true lover's knot, the Bourchier knot, a Tudor rose, a portcullis, a dragon, Christ's wounds, and quaint rebuses, among which are the letter P. with a ram and the letters SAM for " P. Ramsam."

At the west end of the north aisle of the nave is the Saxon door-way, the only remaining part of the great Saxon church which stood on the site. This doorway was reopened, with a covering porch built to preserve it, in 1947 as a thankoffering by the " Friends of Sherborne Abbey " for the preservation of the Abbey during the 1939–45 war.

At the west end of the south aisle is the blocked Norman door which was part cause of the serious rupture between monks and townsfolk described above.

Now passing eastward along the **South Aisle** the buckled Norman arch between the aisle and the transept may be seen. On the right, at the end of the aisle, is **St. Katherine's, or Leweston, Chapel**, containing the tomb of John Leweston (d. 1584) and Joane his wife. Some glass, probably dating from the fifteenth century, has been placed here. This had been taken out of the choir windows in 1856 and placed in the muniment room, where it had remained.

The **South Transept** has a fine roof of dark Irish oak, a Te Deum window designed by A. W. Pugin and monuments of the last Earl of Bristol and other memorials of the Digby family. There is one composed by Alexander Pope, alluding to " moral " by mistake for " mortal " remains.

The **Choir** has been claimed as the most perfect piece of Perpendicular work in existence. Certainly the roof is an unrivalled example of fifteenth-century **Fan Vaulting.** Some of the figures in the clerestory windows represent the bishops and abbots of Sherborne. The fifteenth-century misericords of the choir stalls are notable.

At the entrance to the south choir aisle is the doorway to the **Tower.** (The ascent can be made on application to the verger.) The Tower contains a peal of eight bells, a sanctus bell and a fire bell. The tenor bell is inscribed: —

" By Wolsey's gift I measure time for all.
To mirth, to griefe, to Church I serve to call."

Wolsey, born in 1471 and " fashioned to much honour from the cradle," was tutor to the Marquis of Dorset's sons. He became Bishop of Lincoln, then Archbishop of York, and was created a Lord Cardinal by Pope Leo X. He then became Lord High Chancellor of England. On the revenues of the Bishopric of Tournai being granted to him, he sent seven huge bells to England from the Continent. Great Tom at Sherborne is the smallest. Formerly, this bell needed six men to toll it. The nett weight is 46 cwt. 0 qrs. 23 lb. The bells form the heaviest peal of eight in the country. They were retuned, and Great Tom recast, in 1934.

The *Fire Bell* was rung only on the occasion of a great fire in the town. Its lip turns inwards and the bell emits a most discordant sound. It is inscribed: —

" Lord, quench this furious flame,
Arise, run, help put out the same."

At the west end of the choir aisle, close to the entrance to the tower, is the **Chapel of the Holy Sepulchre.**

In the ambulatory, facing the south choir aisle, is the screen forming the entrance to the *Chapel of Our Lady of Bow.* The base is fourteenth-century and the remainder, beautifully worked in stone in keeping with it, was given by the Dorset Freemasons as a War Memorial. In this chapel is a font made by piecing together parts of two ancient ones. To the north of this, under a fine Early English arch, is the entrance to the **Lady Chapel,** formerly shut off from the Abbey by a wall, and long occupied as a dwelling-house by masters of Sherborne School. The entrance, now beautifully decorated with modern oak linen-fold panelling and carved screens given by the Dorset Regiment, has been converted into a War Memorial Ante-Chapel.

In the floor northward of the Lady Chapel is a brass noting the fact that the Saxon cathedral was the *Burial-place of Ethelbald and Ethelbert,* kings of the west Saxons, and elder brothers of Alfred the Great.

On the east side of the North Transept is the **Wickham Chapel,** containing the fine tomb of *Sir John Horsey* (d. 1546) and his son (d. 1564). At the corner of the canopy are horses' heads, the crest of the family.

To the left of the entrance to the Abbey Close are—

The Almshouses

(**Open** to visitors. Hours 10.30-12, 2.30-4. No charge.)

These were founded in 1437 and house about twenty old men and women. The buildings should really be known as the Hospital of St. John the Baptist and St. John the Evangelist. The original licence from Henry VI is extant. The old building was enlarged in 1858 and again in 1866. Notice the east window of the Board Room, protruding from the wall. The fifteenth-century triptych (one of four in England) was lent to the Exhibition of British Primitive Art at Burlington House in 1923. Other treasures include Jacobean chairs and tables, fifteenth-century glass, a fine carved screen and a magnificent collection of pewter.

The buildings on the western side of the Close are private houses and offices. The house standing back is the Vicarage.

109

Sherborne School

was refounded and endowed as a grammar school by Edward VI in 1550 in continuance of a tradition of education dating back to St. Aldhelm, the first Bishop of Sherborne in 705. It is now a large public school of some 600 boys. But a number of the former monastic buildings survive and have been skilfully incorporated into modern additions; the effect is harmonious and of considerable beauty. A school historian has aptly written about Sherborne: "It is the most venerable of all institutions in this ancient place, with a life of nearly twelve centuries; older than the English realm itself, and but two centuries younger than the first West Saxon settlement in Britain. That is a long story, but it is all written on these buildings for him that has eyes to see."

Sherborne **School for Girls** is a large and flourishing modern institution run on public school lines.

Following northward the main path across the Close, passing between school buildings, then bearing right and soon after-

wards to the left, a narrower street is reached which goes towards the right into **Cheap Street.** Near some beautiful timber-framed buildings in the lower part of the thoroughfare is the **Conduit,** which was origi-nally in the cloisters, where it was no doubt used for the ablu-tions of the monks. "In 1834 its windows were glazed, a door was put to it, and it was furnished at a cost of £140 as a reading-room for the use of the town." It is now windowless and doorless and is used as a shelter. Near the station are the beautiful *Pageant Gardens*, commemorating the historical pageant which Sherborne staged in 1905—the first of these popular entertainments. Up Cheap Street, on the right-hand side, is an ancient building called the Julian and now used as a public library.

Sherborne Old Castle

A picturesque ruin is all that remains of this former palace and stronghold, situated in a fine park on the eastern side of the town.

The ruins may be seen by turning out of Cheap Street into Newland, a thoroughfare by the side of the Digby Estate Office, and notable as the site of Sherborne House, for several years the residence of Macready after his retirement from the stage and recently adapted for the use of Lord Digby's School for Girls. This delightful Georgian house has a beautiful stairway adorned with paintings by Sir James Thornhill. Maclise, the painter, Forster, the biographer, Thackeray and Dickens were constant visitors here. At the bottom of Newland bear to the left for the castle and take the middle road. A good view of the ruins can be obtained by walking a few yards along New Road over the right-hand railway bridge, opposite the *Black Horse Hotel.*

The Castle was built by Bishop Roger of Sarum, who held the diocese from 1107–39. The bishop was one of those who opposed the accession of Stephen. In consequence of this Stephen took the Castle from him in 1139. In 1355 the then Bishop of Salisbury claimed the Castle on the ground that it had been taken from Bishop Roger, only, and not from the see. It was held by the Earl of Salisbury, who appealed to the King for a trial by battle. On the day fixed for the duel the King ordered the Earl to give up the Castle in return for 2,500 marks to be paid by the bishop. Nearly two hundred and fifty years later the estates of the bishop in and near Sherborne were leased to Queen Elizabeth for £200 per annum, and subsequently granted to Sir Walter Raleigh. Owing to a clerical error in the deed of conveyance, this unfortunate courtier was compelled to forfeit the estates to King James, who had promised them to his favourite, Carr. The surrender was not so bad as at first it promised to be, for the King granted substantial monetary compensation. In 1617 the Castle and lands were granted to Sir John Digby, Earl of Bristol.

In 1642 the Castle was besieged by supporters of the Parliament, and stirring scenes were enacted in the streets of Sherborne. When the fortunes of the Civil War favoured the King in the west, Sherborne Castle was a base and rallying-point for the Royalists. In 1645 the Castle was besieged by Fairfax, and in less than a fortnight was taken by storm. Two months later, by order of the Parliament, it was so shattered by gunpowder as to be untenable in future. In 1648 the Earl of Bristol and his son Lord Digby were banished and their estates confiscated. The lands reverted to the Digbys in 1660.

The Modern Castle (privately owned and not open to view) is in the form of the letter H. The middle portion was built by Sir Walter Raleigh. The two wings—the perpendicular strokes of the H—were added after the Restoration of the monarchy.

About three and a half miles to the north-west of Sherborne is the village of **Trent,** with a famous manor house.

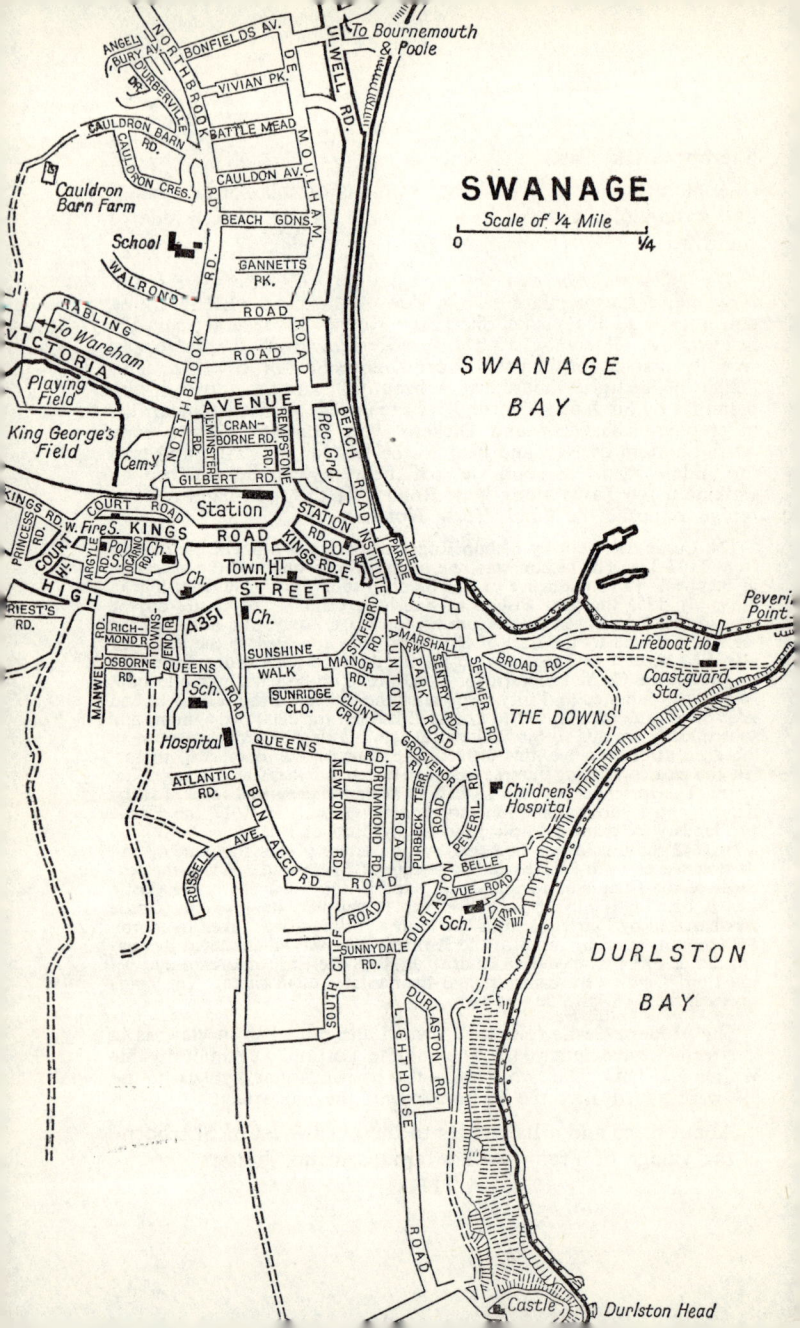

Swanage

Angling.—From the pier and from boats. Frequent local competitions. Fish caught include bass, sole, whiting, mullet, pout, etc.

Banks.—*Lloyds*, High Street; *Midland*, Institute Road; *National Provincial*, Institute Road; *Barclay's*, Station Road.

Bathing.—Safe and good, the front being one long, smooth, gently sloping sandy beach, with at the far northern end an inner fringe of fine shingle. Second or half tides occur at Swanage with the result that there is little difference between high and low water levels. Actually the rise at spring tides is only 6 feet, and at neap tides 3 feet. Huts may be hired.

Boating.—Good boating within the bay. Those who wish to go beyond the headlands are strongly advised to take a boatman as there are strong currents and submerged ledges off Ballard Head and Peveril Point. Swanage Sailing Club have clubhouse close to pier.

Bowls.—There is a green in the Recreation Ground on the seafront.

Buses.—The main bus park is in Victoria Avenue. Services to Studland, Corfe, Wareham and Weymouth. To Bournemouth via Studland, Sandbanks and Canford Cliffs. Variety of **Coach Trips** to all places of interest.

Car Parking.—Limited waiting on certain roads and none on Shore Road. Car parks in Victoria Avenue, Broad Road and De Moulham Road.

Cricket.—Swanage Cricket Club, New Swanage, arrange visitors' matches.

Churches and Chapels.—

St. Mary's Parish Church, King's Road.
St. Aldhelm's, Park Road.
St. Mark's, Bell Street, Herston.
All Saints', New Swanage.
Roman Catholic, Church of Holy Ghost, Victoria Avenue.
Congregational, High Street.
Methodist, High Street and Bell Street.

Baptist, High Street and King's Road, West.
Salvation Army, High Street.
Brethren, Victoria Avenue.
Christian Science, 88 King's Road.
Society of Friends, Rectory Classroom, Church Hill.

Climate.—Dry, mild and bracing. In summer Swanage has the smallest range of temperature on the South Coast. Aspect of the town is east, but northeasterly and northerly winds are broken by hills.

SWANAGE

Distances.—

Anvil Point Lighthouse	. .	2	Kingston	5¼
Ballard Down	. . . . .	2½	Lulworth	17
Bindon Abbey	. . . . .	14	Poole	20
Bournemouth, via ferry	..	12	Studland	4
„ via Wareham		25	Tilly Whim Caves	2
Church Knowle	. . . .	7½	Wareham	10¼
Corfe Castle	. . . . .	6	Wool	15
Durlston Head	. . . . .	1¼	Worth Matravers	4
Kimmeridge	. . . . .	8		

Early Closing.—Thursday.

Entertainment.—Music at sunken bandstand in Recreation Ground. Summer show in Mowlem Theatre, Promenade.

Golf.—The *Isle of Purbeck Golf Club* (18 holes) is situated on the Downs, overlooking Poole Harbour on the north side of the Swanage-Studland Road. Refreshments at Clubhouse. Bus service.

The Dorset Club at Broadstone Heath, a 9-hole course at Wareham, and the municipal courses at Bournemouth are within comparatively easy reach.

*Miniature Golf.—*Charming course opposite pier where hilly ground is cleverly used to offer varied hazards.

Hospital.—Swanage General Hospital, Queen's Road.

Hotels.—*Grosvenor*, Seafront; *Ship*, High Street; *Royal Victoria*, Seafront; *Wolferton*, Victoria Avenue; *Saxmondham*, Burlington Road; *Chatsworth*, Ulwell Road; *Corrie*, De Moulham Road; *Suncliffe*, Burlington Road; *Marston*, Burlington Road; *Grand*, Burlington Road; *York*, Cauldon Avenue; *Pines*, Burlington Road; *Oxford*, Park Road; *Richmond*, Victoria Avenue; and many others.

Library.—Branch of County Library.

Population.—7,800.

Post Office.—Chief office in Station Road. Sub-offices at Court Hill (top of High Street), and at Herston.

Putting.—Green adjoins Beach Tennis Courts. Fine miniature golf course opposite pier.

Sea Trips.—Particulars of boat trips are advertised at the pier.

Tennis.—In Beach Gardens, off De Moulham Road, are nine hard courts available for hire.

The small village of old Swanage with its quaint winding High Street, charming inns and cottages, tiny stone lock-up and thirteenth-century church tower, has expanded into a delightful

114

holiday resort. The beautiful bay, and its fine steep coast, the field paths, magnificent views and glorious windy heaths, delights with its charm and variety.

The **Pier** is situated at the southern end of the bay. The structure is like Swanage itself—pleasant, quiet and unpretentious. It has little resemblance to most piers, being a glorified old-fashioned jetty, 1,400 feet long. There are landing stages for small vessels, the comings and goings of which contribute much to the interest and liveliness of the sea front. At the head are seats and shelters. Anglers may use the pier on payment of the ordinary toll. Adjoining the pier are the remains of a smaller and older structure. It dates from the middle of last century, and was mainly designed to facilitate the shipping of the marble and stone quarried from the neighbouring hills.

The front—as the Parade and Shore Road—provide a pleasant walk and motor road extending for nearly three-quarters of a mile. A granite coloumn on the seafront commemorates an early event in Swanage history. At the base is the inscription: "In commemoration of a great Naval battle fought with the Danes in Swanage Bay by Alfred the Great A.D. 877", but a slight anachronism is introduced by the placing of four cannon balls at its top.

On the inland side of the shore road the **Recreation Ground** occupies a considerable area. Fine views of the bay are obtained from the ridge. There is a tennis court and a popular bowling green while music is provided at a sunken bandstand. On a high part of the ground is the local *War Memorial*, a pile of Purbeck stone. Just beyond the Recreation Ground is a spot called the Spa with a cluster of beach chalets.

Further along the shore road are the *Beach Lawn Tennis Courts*, and here the esplanade comes to an abrupt end, the roadway running off obliquely inland under the name of **Ulwell Road.** Roads leading off to the right of this bring one to the high cliff, with a glorious view over the bay to Peveril Point. The sands can be regained by an easy slope down the cliff face.

To the left of Ulwell Road, in Northbrook Road, is **Day's Park** which includes a football field and stand. Adjoining are the Grammar School grounds and cricket field.

From the Ulwell Road junction one may continue along the shore below the cliffs, passing bathing huts, as far as one pleases towards Ballard Point. This walk is full of interest, while it is possible farther along to link up with the footpath leading over Ballard Down to Studland.

Along the cliff, a short way beyond the Grand Hotel, is the Ballard Estate where are a number of bungalows.

The kernel of Old Swanage is the **High Street,** which, from the *Ship Hotel,* goes uphill towards the Church, traversing the centre of the town from east to west. What is true of Swanage generally is especially true of its High Street—it has " character," an individuality as enduring and sub-stantial as its stone-built and stone-roofed houses. Not that it is all old by any means, but the very medley has been accomplished in a distinctive manner.

Most of the buildings of interest are in or close to the old street. It should be explored on foot, as distances are very short and the narrowness makes stopping and starting of cars awkward.

Half-way up the street, on the right, is the **Town Hall,** with its elaborate façade, which once adorned Mercers' Hall in London. Down the turning by the side of it can be seen, on the left, an even greater curiosity, the **Old Lock-Up,** of stone, " erected," as an inscription unblushingly records, " For the Prevention of Vice and Immorality by the Friends of Religion and good Order, A.D. 1803." The " enemies " of religion and good order at that smug era were apparently the wild quarry boys employed in the neighbourhood.

On the left is **Purbeck House,** with extensive grounds, built by the late Mr. George Burt, the contractor, in 1876, and now used as a convent school. It is said to be on the site of an old monastery of the Monks of Bindon. The tower fronting the street is faced with granite chips from the Albert Memorial,

116

Hyde Park. Many other relics of old London are in the grounds.

Opposite Purbeck House used to stand a picturesque little creeper-covered house known as *Wesley Cottage,* but this was destroyed by enemy action in the Second World War. It was named after John Wesley, who is said to have stayed there at the invitation of Mrs. Mary Burt, when he came to Swanage in 1774, and preached in a meadow to a large congregation.

The road, which has been climbing steadily from the sea-ward end, opens into Church Hill and gives a sudden view of a quaint and beautiful picture. The hill falls away to the right, and we look down upon the sturdy square-towered church, which, however, is but one feature of the delightful whole. To the left is the **Mill Pond,** reflecting picturesque grey, moss-grown stone houses in its quiet waters. At the farther end of the pond is the old mill house, the last of a chain stretching back through centuries—perhaps older than Swanage itself.

A few steps down Church Hill is—

St. Mary's Church,

which, like the mill, has had predecessors, and is said to have been originally a fort. One, and that certainly not the first, was erected in the thirteenth century. The square tower, since added to, is said to be of Saxon origin. It contains a clock and a peal of eight bells, four of which were hung in 1881 by the late Mr. George Burt in memory of his wife. One of the bells dates back to 1594. The church was rebuilt in 1859, and much enlarged in 1908. It provides seating accommodation for about a thousand people. The list of Rectors dates from 1297; there are parish registers, with intermissions, from 1567, and the

handsome service of Communion plate is late seventeenth century.

One of the most famous worthies of Swanage was **Dr. Andrew Bell,** vicar of the town from 1801 to 1810. He was the pioneer, first in India and then at Swanage, of what came to be known as the Madras system of education. Bell had an able colleague in Thomas Manwell, "the Swanage philosopher," and in a short time, with Swanage as a centre, the employment of this system, and of pupil teachers, became a distinctive feature in the educational systems of the country. On leaving Swanage, Dr. Bell became Master of Sherburn House, originally a leper-hospital, near Durham; and when he died he was buried in Westminster Abbey.

There is a very effective view of the Church from the **King's Road,** a level, stream-bordered thoroughfare leading from the station past the **Church Hall** to the more inland parts of the town.

The old **Rectory,** now a private residence, stands on King's Road, and is reached by a little bridge across the stream. It is a most delightful old stone house standing in lovely grounds.

Beyond the Memorial Cross, at the top of Church Hill, Upper High Street becomes still more "high," and a break in the line of buildings on the right gives a glorious view over the town to the long range of Downs that screen it on the north. To the right is Ballard Down (528 ft.), with its white chalk cliffs; then, just below the obelisk, is seen the gap through which winds the road to Studland; next is Round Down, aptly named, scarcely distinguishable, however, from the greater bulk of Nine Barrow Down (655 ft.) extending westward for some miles to the gap commanded by Corfe Castle.

Historical Note

The monument on the Front serves as a reminder that Swanage has a considerable past. It is mentioned in Domesday as *Swanic* and *Swanwick*. In 877 the Danes, who had taken Wareham two years previously, were obliged to retreat to Exeter, some going by sea, the rest marching overland. The fleet was overtaken by Alfred near Swanage, and a great battle took place, in which the Danes were defeated with heavy loss. Still further misfortune befell them, for more than a hundred of their galleys that had survived the fight were driven by a storm on to the rocks of Peveril Point. It is this historic sea-fight—the first considerable naval victory of the English—which is commemorated by the monument. C. E. Robinson incidentally alludes to the event in his *Wreck of the Golden Hind*.

After this time the town itself does not appear to have had an eventful history, being far removed from the lines of march of armies.

Leland, in the time of Henry VIII, refers to it as a " fisher town with a peere and a little fresh water," and in fishing and quarrying its whole history, social as well as economic, has been bound up. The quarrymen, of whom more later, are almost a race apart, with many curious manners and customs, while such an important invention as that of the chain cable is supposed to have been made by a local blacksmith early in the nineteenth century, for hauling the stone out of the quarries.

With the houses almost literally part of the ground they stand on, it is natural that there should have developed an intense local patriotism, in many cases, notably in the Mowlem and Burt families, expressing itself in the development and beautifying of the town.

Swanage owes a great deal to these families. The late Mr. George Burt, who came of a race of quarriers, was a Swanage man and a member of the firm of Mowlem and Co. It was owing to the nature of their contracting work that the firm had the opportunity of acquiring discarded fragments of old London with which to adorn Swanage. (Lamp-posts on the seafront were from London but have since been replaced.) Bringing into play his engineering knowledge and experience, Mr. Burt laid out miles of roads on the estate he acquired around Durlston Head to the west of Swanage Bay. It was he who caused the Great Globe, one of the chief sights of the locality, to be cut out of eight huge blocks of stone, and placed on Durlston Head. Mr. Burt's will laid down that his estate should not be sold until twenty-one years after his death. When this period elapsed, in the summer of 1919, the stone model of the earth was acquired by a private company, together with the famous Tilly Whim Caves.

Since linking up with the railway at Wareham, some sixty years ago, Swanage has changed from the small fishing-quarrying village, of which the narrow old High Street is almost the only unaltered relic, to a pleasant town with private and boarding-houses and hotels standing in pretty gardens and spread over the charming country round the Bay.

Excursions from Swanage

On account of the vast amount of unenclosed heath and downland, walking presents a very great pleasure, and an infinite variety of walks can be enjoyed with ever-changing views to delight the eyes. In spring, summer and autumn the country is almost equally lovely, with a wonderful range of colour and grace of line as well as the beauty of old buildings to give focus to the landscape. At the risk of being considered pedantic, we would repeat the warning given elsewhere of the danger of slipping on the short dry grass near the edge of the cliffs.

Motorists will find most of the main roads excellent, secondary roads surprisingly good, but there are some where the surface is poor. Some over the cliff hills—such as that to Kimmeridge from Corfe—are closed to heavy traffic.

Another point which private drivers should bear in mind is that many of the roads over the cliffs—for example, to Swyre Head—and the low moorlands round Poole Harbour peter out to nothingness. Of course, if time and destination are no object, this does not really matter, and most delightful go-as-you-please walk-rides can be found in spots almost as lonely as the heart of Africa.

With the exception of the gently undulating Valley Road from Swanage to Corfe, which opens up the inland country, gradients are fairly steep. This is the case with the hill road to Corfe, where there is a long pull up out of Swanage through Langton, and a steep twisting road down into Corfe.

I.—TO PEVERIL POINT

The strong tidal flow over Peveril Ledge makes bathing dangerous and boats should take great care.

Peveril Point is the low headland forming the southern horn of Swanage Bay. It is approached by the road overlooking the Pier (passing the back of the *Grosvenor Hotel*). Extending from it is quite a long range of outliers of the Purbeck stone, making a natural groyne of great utility in the protection of Swanage from the tidal forces surging up the Channel. On the cliff is a Coastguard Station which is manned when the weather is rough. Here, too, is a rocket apparatus. Below the cliff, on the northern side, are the old Coastguards' Station, a group of white-washed cottages, and the **Lifeboat House** (*open daily 9–5 except Saturday afternoons and Sundays*). Close by stands the **Clock Tower,** prominent in all views of the town. It is, in fact, a medieval Gothic tower which formerly ornamented the south side of London Bridge, and from which the clock has long disappeared. The boulder-strewn foreshore around the Point forms a delightful place in which to laze, sheltered from sun or wind. In rough weather it is wonderful to watch the sea rushing over the half-submerged rocks that were doubtless good dry land at the time when, according to a discredited tradition, King Alfred defeated the Danes off this very spot. At low tide it is possible to scramble along the rough rocks in the direction of Durlston Head. Many of the rocks are simply masses of oyster-shell conglomerate. Owing to the inclination of the strata, the Purbeck beds, higher, middle and lower, are successively shown in the cliffs between Durlston Bay and Peveril Point, though broken by several faults. At the base of Peveril Point large lumps of gypsum are found. It is dangerous to bathe here.

Several paths intersect the green down south of the Point and can be followed by those who wish to reach Durlston Head and Tilly Whim. It is worth while in any case to climb the brow for the spacious view of Swanage Bay, backed by the long ridge of Ballard Down.

II.—TO DURLSTON HEAD, TILLY WHIM CAVES, GREAT GLOBE AND ANVIL POINT

Buses leave the Pier for Durlston Head and Anvil Point Lighthouse at hourly intervals daily during the season. The drive is very pleasant, but all who have time should walk. From the lower part of High Street ascend either Park Road or Seymer Road.

At the top of Seymer Road a pleasant route can be taken by entering the gate on the left and then going upwards over Peveril Down. Where further progress is barred, enter the

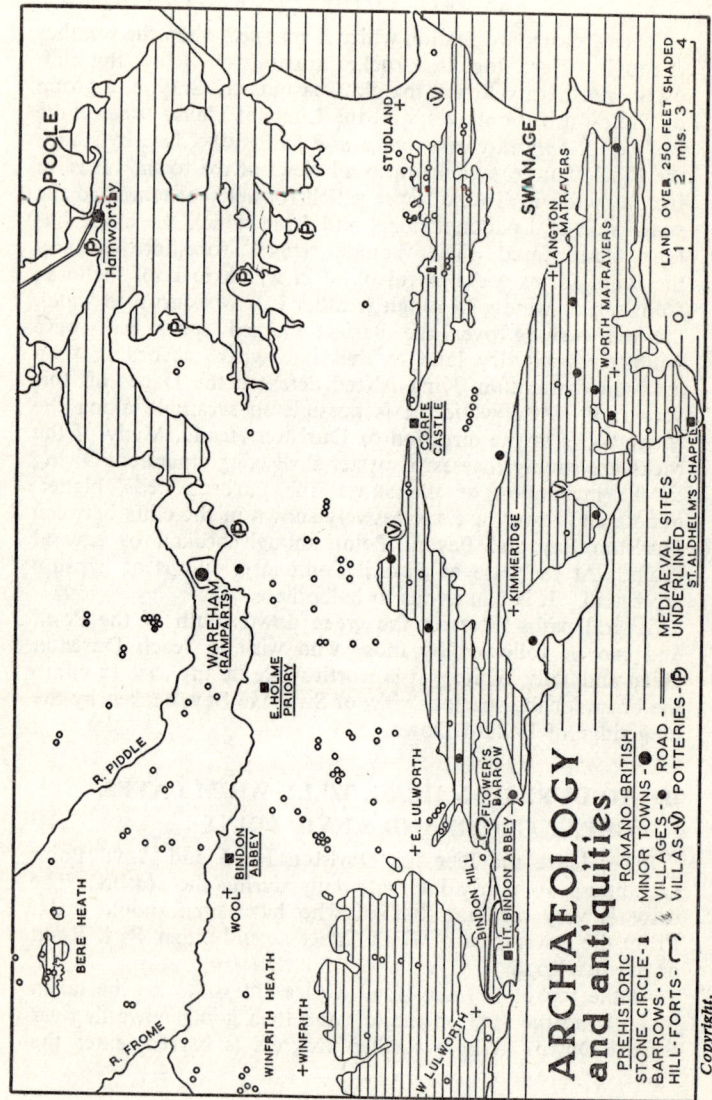

ARCHAEOLOGY and antiquities

POOLE

SWANAGE

BERE HEATH

R. PIDDLE

Hamworthy

STUDLAND

WAREHAM (RAMPARTS)

E. HOLME PRIORY

CORFE CASTLE

+ LANGTON MATRAVERS

WORTH MATRAVERS

+ KIMMERIDGE

+ ST. ALDHELMS CHAPEL

R. FROME

WINFRITH HEATH

+ WINFRITH

WOOL + BINDON ABBEY

+ E. LULWORTH

FLOWER'S BARROW

BINDON HILL

LIT. BINDON ABBEY

+ W. LULWORTH

PREHISTORIC
STONE CIRCLE - ▲
BARROWS - o o
HILL-FORTS - ⌒

ROMANO-BRITISH
MINOR TOWNS - ■
VILLAGES - ●
VILLAS - ⌒
POTTERIES - Ⓟ

ROAD - ...

MEDIAEVAL SITES
UNDERLINED

LAND OVER 250 FEET SHADED
0   1   2   3   4
                  mls.   mls.

road on the right. A few yards ahead is the *Tilly Whim Inn,* which is reached also by the high road.

Durlston Head, the southern horn of Swanage Bay, is only a mile from Swanage. Near it is *Durlston Castle,* an imposing modern structure of Purbeck stone, used as a restaurant and appearing to be of more consequence. Paths lead down to an enclosure (*admission charge*) in which stands—

The Great Globe,

of Portland stone, 10 ft. in diameter and forty tons in weight, provided by the late Mr. George Burt. It is so poised as to represent the position of the earth in space, and on it are shown in slight relief the chief divisions of the earth's surface. Stone benches around indicate the eight chief points of the compass, and massive slabs provide a variety of information on the subject of earth, sun, moon and stars, and appropriate quotations from ancient and modern authors. In the hope of preserving the globe and tablets from defacement by the amateur carver, two large slabs are provided for those who *must* leave their autographs behind.

From the Globe the bird-haunted cliff path, 102 ft. above sea-level, continues south-westward to—

The Tilly Whim Caves

(**Admission,** charge.)

At one part the path descends a dark and steep tunnel cut obliquely through the solid rock. It is an eerie entrance, and leads abruptly into the first of the two caves, which have been described as " like nothing on earth so much as an Egyptian rock temple." The tunnel has been closed by a gate and one of the caves has been closed by a wall. The caves are the remains of a quarry, in which working ceased about a century ago. At one time they were doubtless found useful by smugglers. They have been said to owe their curious name to having been the " whim " of a man named Tilly. A more reasonable explanation represents Tilly as a man of wisdom, not of folly. In the West Country, " whim " is the name of any mechanical contrivance for raising or lowering the produce of mines, and such machines being rare in the neighbourhood of Swanage, Tilly's quarry became known as Tilly Whim, after the new-fangled crane by which the stone was lowered over the cliff.

Tilly Whim is a favourite resort of picnic parties in summer weather, but it should also be visited during a gale from the south-west, for then the waves break majestically over the rocks, flinging great columns of spray in all directions. The bold rock scenery along this part of the coast is almost unique. The rocks are high, jagged and fearsome, dangerous for boats in rough weather. On

123

the water-worn terraces formed by the sea, the rocks are a conglomerate of shells, weather-hardened, and water-worked by the tremendous force of the tides beating and dragging, tearing and driving continually on them.

The Portland Oolite begins to show in Durlston Bay, and not far from where this is observed it will be found that the Purbeck stone has merged into the limestone.

Returning to the higher level, a footpath leads a short distance along the cliff to **Anvil Point,** so-called because just above high-water mark is a small anvil-shaped rock. Visitors are permitted to see the lantern and other features of the Lighthouse on week-days from 1 p.m. to an hour before sunset. In August there is usually quite a long queue and the keepers are kept busy. The two pylons close by mark the end of a measured mile used for sea speed trials.

If time permits, good walkers can extend the excursion as far as they please in the direction of **St. Aldhelm's Head** (p. 133). The coast-watcher's path is plainly marked, and there is a superb view all along, not only of the bold and rugged coast, but inland over the Purbeck valley to Ballard Down and Nine Barrow Down.

Nearly midway between Anvil Point and St. Aldhelm's Head is the **Dancing Ledge,** a gently inclining platform of stone of uneven and varying shape. This at certain high tides gives rise to a dancing action of the waves. The rugged scenery is magnificent, and the Ledge is a favourite picnic spot. Immediately after it is left, St. Aldhelm's Head is seen standing out in bold and massive strength, catching the full force of the south-west waves. The rocks here are identical with those at Portland, sixteen miles away.

The return from the headland to Swanage could be made by turning inland to Worth Matravers (p. 130) and back by the hill road, a round of about eleven miles. A bus could be picked up at Worth Matravers or Langton.

III.—TO BALLARD DOWN AND OLD HARRY ROCKS

A walk there and back of about six miles, including a somewhat steep hill climb. This walk should not be missed, for the double view from the top of Ballard Down is one of the finest even in this county of fine views.

The route is easy to follow. Proceed northward along the Esplanade to where the Ulwell Road leaves the Front. Continue until the road turns to the left preparatory to climbing the Downs by an easy ascent. At the turning-point leave the road and pass through a new estate on the right; after crossing fields, a path ascends to **Whitecliff Farm.** A cottage stands beside the path. The farm-house lies a little to the east (the right) of the path. It is an Elizabethan building, surrounded by fine old elms and poplars.

The track—very sticky in wet weather—now runs between high banks, ascending somewhat steeply to the open down. (The footpath continuing due north over the hill leads down to *Woodhouse,* a quarter of a mile west of Studland.) For Studland and Ballard Point, bear rightward, reaching on the crest of the ridge (here 449 ft. above sea-level) a stone seat aptly incised *" Rest and be Thankful."*

Those who are reserving Studland for another excursion should continue eastward from *Rest and be Thankful,* along the bare crest of the ridge, to **Ballard Point,** a bold chalk promontory, with vertical walls, presenting a fine specimen of the "White Cliffs of Old England." It has an elevation of 382 ft., and forms the northern extremity of Swanage Bay. A warning note is necessary—the grassy slopes leading to the cliff edge are very steep and slippery, and this applies almost more when they are sun-baked than when wet. Nasty accidents have happened both here and on the loose, stony slopes which form so prominent a feature from the sea-front.

A mile north-east of Ballard Point is the **Foreland,** or Handfast Point, below which will be seen the **Old Harry Rocks,** pillars of chalk, forming well-known landmarks. Winds and waves are telling on them. "Old Harry" suffered considerable loss of dignity during a severe gale in 1896, while his consort was nearly demolished. The rocks are better seen from a boat than from the land. Those familiar with Thomas Hardy's *Hand of Ethelberta* will recall the description of the rough steamboat journey from Sandbourne (Bournemouth) to Knollsea (Swanage), and of the still rougher return journey, past the "windy, sousing, thwacking, basting, scourging Jack Ketch of a corner called Old Harry Point, which lay about midway along the track, and stood with its detached posts and stumps of white rock like a skeleton's lower jaw grinning at British Navigation!"

From Ballard Point the return to Swanage can be varied by making for the cliff-path, which presently descends to the shore some distance north of New Swanage.

IV.—TO STUDLAND
Postal Address, Studland, Swanage, Dorset.

This is easily the favourite excursion from Swanage. There is a frequent bus service, while for walkers there is the footpath over the Downs. Cars take the Ulwell Road, which winds through the gap between Ballard Down and Nine Barrow Down. The drive (3½ miles) is pleasant, but of course misses the marvellous double view from the crest of Ballard Down. It is a good plan to take a bus one way and walk the other. The distance by the footpath route is two and three-quarter miles.

The footpath route is as described in the last excursion to the *Rest and be Thankful* seat at the top of Ballard Down. From this point, the path descends obliquely in a north-easterly direction to a well-beaten track leading directly to Studland. At the entrance to the village is a remnant of the old *Cross*. Here there is a choice of three routes.

To the right the picturesque Watery Lane, reminiscent of Guernsey, leads to the shore. At low tide it is possible to continue along the sands, round Redend Point, to the northern part of the village and the open greensward bordering the sea to Haven Point. The road to the left from the Cross runs past the rectory, and the third to the church.

A footpath runs from the north-east corner of the churchyard to a tree-shaded road in which stands the *Bankes Arms Hotel* towards the right and the picturesque *Manor House Hotel* towards the left. Motorists enter the village on the west, and take the first turning to the right past the Post Office for the Church Cross and Hotel. Cars may be parked in certain fields (*charge*).

Studland is one of the prettiest villages in England, and is as yet almost unspoilt. Perfect in itself, it is also perfect in its setting—woodland, sea and downland combining in a picture of rare charm. Its day population is always largely recruited from Bournemouth and Swanage. The bathing is excellent, and the 18-hole course of the Isle of Purbeck Golf Club (*see* p. 114) is within easy reach.

The **church** (8, 11, 6.30) is dedicated to St. Nicholas of Myra, the patron saint of sailors. It is " a singularly perfect and unaltered specimen of Norman style, and may well rank with the well-known churches of Iffley and Stewkley."

" Its date is somewhat earlier than Iffley, perhaps about 1180. The whole is of this period with very few exceptions, consisting of modern alterations. The plan is a nave, central tower and chancel, the two latter with stone-groined roof. The east window is an insertion of three lights of late date, perhaps Jacobean. Above (seen from the outside) is the original window between the two roofs. There are original north and south windows, each a narrow light with good exterior mouldings and a wide splay. On the north side of the Sanctuary is a Purbeck marble altar tomb of the fifteenth century.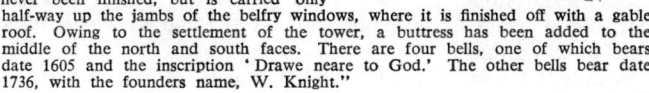
" In the tower the north window is original, the south modern. The tower has never been finished, but is carried only half-way up the jambs of the belfry windows, where it is finished off with a gable roof. Owing to the settlement of the tower, a buttress has been added to the middle of the north and south faces. There are four bells, one of which bears date 1605 and the inscription ' Drawe neare to God.' The other bells bear date 1736, with the founders name, W. Knight."

The water of the wide and quiet bay of Studland is too shallow for any but small vessels. The cliffs are of sand coloured with iron, as are those exactly opposite, at Alum Bay, in Isle of Wight, and it can easily be understood, as one looks across, how at one time the intervening miles were land instead of water. The sand dunes along the shore are very popular with picnic parties, and bear an abundance of wild flowers. There is a charming view of the Hampshire Coast and the Isle of Wight. Many acres of this heathland are now a nature reserve. It is also a pleasant walk by the low shore northward to South Haven, where a ferry crosses the mouth of Poole Harbour to North Haven, for Canford Cliffs and Branksome.

As already stated, new and excellent roads go from Studland to South Haven and from Sandbanks, across the water, to Bournemouth, a sturdy **ferry** usefully connecting those two roads. The construction of the roads is greatly changing the appearance of these formerly remote corners, has reduced the distance from Bournemouth to Swanage by something like 15 miles, and has opened up some of the most charming scenery on the south coast.

A popular picnic place in this vicinity is **Shell Bay.**

Of the walks from Studland, one is that to—

The Agglestone

(*i.e., Holy Stone*), a huge mass of ironstone on a little hillock, amid the region of boggy moorland which lies between the village and the creeks of Poole Harbour. The distance from Studland is only about a mile. The road running northward from the village towards Knoll House Hotel should at first be taken. In a few yards turn up a by-way to the left towards the riding stables and follow a continuing track across the moor. The stone will shortly be seen some distance to the left. It is about 17 ft. high, and is estimated to weigh fully four hundred tons.

A little to the north is a similar but smaller block known as the **Puckstone.**

V.—TO CORFE

Corfe is usually reached by train, bus or coach, or by the wonderful six-mile walk over the hills described below.

Follow Victoria Avenue from the Front, across Northbrook Road, to a point a short distance west of the railway station, where a footpath will be seen on the right (*see* our plan). This leads across several meadows to **Godlingston Farm** (1¾ miles). A glimpse of the exterior of the house is alone worth the walk, for the building is a delightful specimen of English domestic architecture, in its

128

Swanage *(John T. Etches)*

Swanage Bay and Ballard Down *(John T. Etches)*

The Great Globe (*Valentine*)

Tilly Whim Caves (*John T. Etches*)

shelter of trees. Parts date from the fourteenth century or earlier. An ancient portion is a semicircular turret at the western end of the front with walls over 4 feet thick.

On emerging into the lane opposite the farm, turn for a few yards to the right, along the Godlingston road, and a gate will be seen on the left, giving access to a path which skirts the east side of the farm and its delightful gardens and presently joins the footpath ascending **Nine Barrow Down** (655 ft.). Once on the ridge directions are unnecessary. There is a glorious view across the valley to the quarry-scarred heights to the south, and by diverging a little northward from the path the whole expanse of Poole Harbour, with Bournemouth beyond, is visible. From Nine Barrow Down the route passes without a break to **Brenscombe Hill,** the path gradually descending to Corfe, the village being entered close to the station. The finest possible view of the Castle ruins is obtained from **Challow Hill,** which overlooks them from a height of nearly 400 ft. Though comparatively little known, this is one of the finest walks in Dorset. The invigorating air at this height and the springy nature of the turf make walking a real delight. The return could be made by train or bus. For **Corfe,** *see* pp. 140-144.

If there is plenty of time a longer hill-top route could be used by first ascending Ballard Down, as described on p. 125, turning inland at the *Rest and be Thankful* seat and continuing along the crest to the *Obelisk* above the water-works at Ulwell. Here it is necessary to descend, on account of the gap in the hills. Or the walk could be started from the Gap, on the Ulwell Road. After crossing the Ulwell Road, a continuing footpath will be seen which skirts the southern foot of **Round Down** (300 ft.) and then slopes gradually up to the ridge of Nine Barrow Down, being joined by the footpath already indicated.

VI.—TO THE PURBECK QUARRIES

Herston—Langton Matravers—Worth Matravers—The Quarries

Swanage High Street is continued by the Herston Road, which soon passes, on the right, **Newton Manor,** one of the old manor houses for which the Swanage and Purbeck country is famous. It has, however, retained only fragments of the original structure. Over the gateway is a weather-vane believed to have come from Billingsgate. The kitchen has an Elizabethan stone fire-place (now covered over), and the old barn, with an open timber roof, has been made into a dining-hall, which has a fine open fire-place built of Purbeck stone. This beautiful old house was for a quarter of a century the home of Sir John Charles Robinson, C.B. (d. 1913), founder of the South Kensington Art Department, who here gathered a choice collection of treasures.

On the left is soon passed a short turning leading uphill to *St. Mark's Church,* serving the western part of Swanage and Herston, once a tiny village of quarry workers, but now rapidly developing with new housing estates.

Beyond Herston the road forks left and rises steeply to the summit of Steppeshill with a panoramic view of the straggling village of—

Langton Matravers,

about two and a half miles from the Swanage front. To the long street (Saxon " long-tun ") of stone cottages and an occasional fine house have now been added several housing estates on the seaward side. The village has for many years been known for its excellent preparatory schools. The **Church,** dedicated to St. George, was built in 1876, with the exception of the tiny tower, lower than the body of the church, which is probably 700 years old. The registers date from 1670, and the rectors of the parish can be traced in unbroken succession to the year 1290. Near the church is a rectory, a portion of which is very old, and contains a " Priest's Oven " which may have been used for baking the Sacramental Bread. In front of the house is a sundial, from the porch of the church.

Almost opposite the church a lane leads to **Dancing Ledge,** with its swimming bath hewn from the rock (*see* p. 124). On the cliffs to the south, in the valley, and on Nine Barrow Down to the north are some delightful walks.

From Langton Matravers the main road continues to **Kingston** (p. 134). Follow it for about a mile and then turn left to—

Worth Matravers,

once a more important little place. Stone-quarrying is carried on by the greater number of its male inhabitants. The

Church, dedicated, like that of Studland, to St. Nicholas of Myra, is said to have been begun in the year 700 by the Saxon King Ine. Part of the old building can be seen adjoining the tower. The Normans were responsible for considerable additions, and the church is of great archaeological and artistic interest. Its good features include a twelfth-century chancel arch, a credence table, and a piscina. In the churchyard a tombstone commemorates the pioneer of vaccination, one Benjamin Jesty, a farmer who lived at the neighbouring *Downshay Manor House*, a Jacobean building. His epitaph reads:—

" *Sacred* to the memory of Benjm. Jesty of Downshay, who departed this Life April 10th, 1810, aged 79 years.

" He was born at Yetminster in this *County* and was an upright honest man particularly *modest* for having been the first Person known that introduced the Cow Pox by *inoculation and* who from his great *strength of mind* made the Experiment from the *Cow* on his Wife and two Sons."

The chief inn bears the appropriate sign of the Square and Compass, and possesses a lightning sketch of the late proprietor by Mr. Augustus John.

About a mile and a half south of Worth Matravers is **St. Aldhelm's Head** (p. 133).

Langton Matravers and Worth Matravers are the largest of the quarry villages upon the hills at the back of Swanage. The hills are scored with hundreds of little quarries. Rough roads and rougher cart tracks cross the downs in every direction, leading to the villages in which the quarriers live. To those who are familiar with the big open quarries worked by large firms—

The Purbeck Quarries

seem very primitive. No objection is likely to be raised to anyone visiting these family quarries, and frequently the men will show fossils found in working the stone, and explain the methods used.

Two or three men own and work a quarry. According to ancient custom, no stranger is allowed to enter into partnership with a native, and all workers must have served an apprenticeship of seven years in the " Ancient Order of Purbeck Marblers and Stonecutters." This is one of the oldest trade unions in the country, sharing with the Borough of Corfe a charter granted by Queen Elizabeth, which entitled Corfe to two seats in Parliament. The formal apprenticeship system is dying out, if not already dead, and some of the other customs have undergone some modification. The industry is still controlled and regulated annually by the workers. They have the power to inflict penalties, but the accused may appeal to an open meeting of the quarrymen. Every Shrove Tuesday the Quarries' Guild meets at Corfe, where general business is transacted. In the past, at this meeting apprentices who had served their full seven years were admitted as fully-fledged members, or " free men," on each bringing to the warden a small loaf of bread and a bottle of beer, together with the prescribed fee of 6s. 8d. One of the articles of the guild, and one that is still rigidly upheld, is that not even a day's work shall be given to a non-member. The most important right claimed by the marblers, the right to enter on any man's land and work the stone, has not been conceded for many years, though a short time ago one tried to do so and was punished for trespass.

Although Purbeck stone is in but little favour with modern architects as a building stone, owing to the small size of the blocks, a good deal of quarrying of stone for other purposes is still carried on, and once a year a pound of pepper and a football are presented to the manorial lords of Ower Quay, at which much of the stone was shipped. The football is reminiscent of the Shrove Tuesday game at Corfe in Middle Halves, a portion of an immense field having also its East and West Halves. The football is carried by the last member to be married during the year.

VII.—TO ST. ALDHELM'S HEAD

The most attractive route is undoubtedly that indicated on p. 121 to Durlston Head and Anvil Point and then on by the cliff path, a total distance out and home of about fourteen miles. The walking distance can be shortened some four miles by taking the cliff path in one direction only and for the other journey making use of the bus service on the road passing through Langton Matravers.

Those who drive take at first the hill road for Corfe, which leaves Swanage by High Street and beyond the town runs through Herston and Langton Matravers (p. 130). From the latter can be seen, across the turf-covered height, the little chapel on the summit of St. Aldhelm's Head, and the neighbouring Coastguards' Station. The Downs have a curious terrace formation up their sides, the " Lynchets," of unknown origin, but possibly relics of some ancient method of agriculture. Similar terraces are seen in the Berkshire Downs. Pedestrians can cut across the grass, or follow the paths.

St. Aldhelm's Head,

also marked on maps as St. Alban's Head, is named after Aldhelm, first bishop of Sherborne, who received his appointment in the eighth century (p. 106). The situation is very lonely, for the great cliff, nearly 400 ft. high, seems anxious to get as far out to sea as possible. It is the most prominent feature of the coast between Swanage and Weymouth. From the extreme point it sends out a ridge of terrible rocks on which many a ship has been wrecked and many a life lost. The view on every side is magnificent.

The massively constructed and heavily buttressed **Chapel,** which also bears St. Aldhelm's name, is a mystery so far as its origin is concerned. There is a theory that it was erected by one of the early kings who occasionally resided at Corfe Castle, and in support of the theory there is the fact that the chapel was anciently served by a royal chaplain. Then there is also a tradition that the chapel was erected in 1140 by a sorrowing father who witnessed the drowning off the Head of his daughter and her bridegroom.

The edifice, architecturally Norman, is square in plan and the walls are very low. It is entered by a Norman doorway and is lighted by a single deeply-splayed window. The stone roof rises from each side to the centre, where it is flattened: here are remains of a circular turret which may have supported a beacon. The Latin cross which now surmounts the apex of the roof is modern. The interior of the roof is vaulted with the ribs springing from a central column of abnormal thickness. Young romantics leave a pin in a hole of this column while they mentally register a wish. The building is still used for an occasional service.

From St. Aldhelm's Head there is a way down to **Chapman's Pool** (p. 134) on the west side, but the track is steep and rough, and at one point gives place to a scramble down an almost perpendicular cliff.

On the cliff path from Durlston Head to St. Aldhelm's is a small patch of level ground, East Man, between *Winspit* and *Seacombe Cliff,* where are the graves of unfortunate passengers drowned when the East Indiaman *Halsewell* was wrecked in 1786. Charles Dickens in later years wrote, in *The Long Voyage,* a vivid account of this disaster.

All along this part of the coast the cliffs are riddled with quarryings. Specially notable is Winspit Quarry, which consists of a terrace and several subterranean cavities.

VIII.—TO KINGSTON

Kingston, four and a half miles from Swanage and two from Corfe, is on a bus route. The road has been described to a point a mile beyond Langton Matravers (p. 130). Approaching Kingston from Corfe, one of the footpaths leading over Corfe Common can be taken.

The pretty village of **Kingston,** screened with woods and standing at a height of over 400 feet, is seen far and wide. It is remarkable for its elaborate **Church,** built at a cost of £60,000 by the third Lord Eldon in 1880, from designs by Street. A great deal of Purbeck marble from Lord Eldon's quarries was used in the interior. Monuments to the family here were removed from the old church built by Lord Chancellor Eldon, and which is now used as parish hall. About a mile to the south is an obelisk erected to the memory of Lord Stewell, brother of John Scott, first Earl of Eldon, and Lord Chancellor for 25 years, whose family still live at Encombe House, about 1½ miles south of Kingston, in the valley known as the *Golden Bowl* by reason of the fertility of the soil.

Also a short distance from Kingston are the remains of the old manor house of **Scowles,** where may be seen portions of a thirteenth-century building, thought to have been used as a chapel.

From Kingston, too, a rough motor road leads southward for about a mile and a half to **Chapman's Pool.**

From Kingston, by keeping on past the new church instead of turning to the right for Corfe, there is a way to the open down country of **Swyre Head.**

Go through a gateway, known as London Doors, on Encombe Farm and follow a rough road (possible for cars in fairly dry weather) for 1½ miles to Swyre Head. Walkers have right of way, but a toll is charged for cars to Swyre Head in summer.

IX.—TO CHAPMAN'S POOL

The Pool is a lonely cove near the foot of St. Aldhelm's Head, on the west side. "A miniature Lulworth Cove," it has been called, but the Pool lies between cliffs of sombre blackness, due to the presence of Kimmeridge clay, and the scene is very desolate. Kimmeridge coal (so called) found in the black clay, was at one time burned in local homes. The beach is strewn with shaly rocks and boulders; and hundreds of cormorants nest in the rocks.

Many fossils can be found in the vicinity. (*See* p. 149.)

There is bathing, boating and very good fishing, but as there is no inn at the Pool, those who visit it must take their refreshments with them.

A visit to the Pool can be combined with a visit to Kingston (p. 135) and of course the Pool can be reached from St. Aldhelm's Head (but *see* p. 133), from which there is an under-cliff path. A route often taken is through Worth Matravers (p. 130), past the very ancient *Renscombe Farm*, and along the picturesque and leafy *Renscombe Vale*. There is a toll-gate at the bottom of Renscombe Hill, the road leading to a car park above the Pool.

Some combine a visit to the Pool with a visit to Corfe, which can be reached by train or bus. From Corfe go across Corfe Common to the Kingston Road, then up the steep hill to the last bend in the road before the village is reached. Thence the route is through the gate on the left and towards the old church. The field is left by a gate against the churchyard, and another entered on the opposite side of the road. The way lies across this field, in the same southerly direction, an adjacent cricket-field, two more fields, and then to the left, past half a dozen cottages. Past the last cottage on the right, and through a gate, a turn to the right leads direct to the Pool.

X.—TO BOURNEMOUTH

Boat trips.—Excursions during the summer months. The distance by water is about eight miles.

Road and Rail.—The journey by rail has to be made *viâ* Wareham, a round-about route of twenty-five miles. By road *viâ* South Haven-Sandbanks *ferry* (11 miles), or *viâ* Wareham and round Poole Harbour (25 miles).

The short boat trip across Swanage Bay affords a fine view of the town and the background of hills. The white cliffs of Ballard Point and the Foreland are well displayed, and whether in sun or storm always present a grand and imposing sight. Prominent, too, are the **Old Harry Rocks,** but the charming village of Studland is almost screened from view by foliage. A long, low spit of land nearly encloses Poole Harbour. Then come Canford Cliffs, Branksome Chine, Alum Chine, distinguished by its suspension bridge, and Durley Chine. A full description of Bournemouth is given in our *Red Guide to Bournemouth*.

XI.—TO THE NEW FOREST

Guide Book.—Our *Guide to the New Forest* contains special maps and plans and particulars of walks, etc., in the Forest and of the many points in Southampton which should not be overlooked.

Railway Stations.—The most convenient stations for those wishing to see typical New Forest scenery are *Brockenhurst, Lyndhurst Road* (3 miles from Lyndhurst—motor services) and *Beaulieu Road*, midway between the two. Keen walkers may be recommended to alight at, say, Brockenhurst and go *viâ* Queen's Bower and Mark Ash to Minstead and the Rufus Stone, returning *viâ* Lyndhurst and Lyndhurst Road Station.

Road Route.—A popular circular tour passes through **Wareham** and **Wimborne** and on to the little town of **Ringwood,** beyond which the Forest is entered, but a more direct way from Swanage is by the car-ferry to Sandbanks and so *viâ* Bournemouth to Christchurch or Ringwood. *Viâ* Picket Post and Stoney Cross the high road passes close to the *Rufus Stone*, marking the traditional spot where William II fell.

XII.—TO SALISBURY

The excursion to the New Forest is often combined with a visit to Salisbury, but the ancient cathedral city deserves more than a hurried half-hour. Those who do find they have time to spare after seeing its sights might well go on to **Old Sarum,** the original site of Salisbury (the official designation of the local municipality still refers to " New Sarum "), and to Stonehenge.

From Swanage to Salisbury the route is *viâ* Wareham and Blandford; those who cross Poole Harbour by the ferry have a shorter route *viâ* Ringwood and Fordingbridge.

Our *Guide to the New Forest* contains plans and maps and a full description not only of Salisbury but of **Old Sarum,** 1¼ miles northward, and of **Stonehenge,** 11 miles from Salisbury.

XIII.—POOLE HARBOUR

This lovely stretch, with its beautiful surroundings, has been called the **Lakeland of Dorset,** and in miniature it does seem to reproduce the lakeland of Cumberland and Westmorland

—not, of course, with bold and stern mountain scenery and large lakes, but with softer and smaller outlines.

Poole Harbour shows how the action of water has shaped, and is still shaping, this corner of the Dorset coast. The sea is constantly wearing away the sand-cliffs which connect Dorset with Hampshire, and carrying the spoil to the sand-bar outside the Harbour, making a natural protection for the strip of land known as **Sandbanks.** Much sand and silt is also carried by the sea into the Harbour, but the rivers Frome and Piddle, which empty themselves into the backwaters of the inlet, are now the chief agents in the silting-up process, which is slowly but surely taking place. Years ago the port was Wareham. Now the eight-mile passage there can only be used by small boats owing to the constant accumulation of debris. The Harbour is always lovely, whether uncovered by the tide and with the long, sandy reaches sparkling in the sunshine, or with the tide up, filling the channels of the rivers and streams, and all the bays and creeks set in their lovely surroundings of tiny cliffs, clumps of trees, flowering heather and glittering sandy beaches of the long coast. It is perhaps at its most beautiful at sunset, with the pools reflecting a flaming light and the dark mass of the Purbecks brooding behind.

Exclusive of all islands, the area of this vast sea-lake is 10,000 acres, and the length of the coast-line is more than 100 miles. Every third year in summer, the Mayor, the City Fathers and a jury of watermen proceed to beat the bounds of Poole Harbour, as in ancient times. At certain selected spots an old charter is read claiming jurisdiction "over land, water, fish and folk." Within the Harbour and near the entrance is—

Brownsea Island

(originally Bruno's ey), sometimes called Branksea. It is about one and a half miles long by three-quarters broad and has an area of about 500 acres. Its sides are covered with fir groves, while the interior is broken up into miniature glens and hills, some rising to a height of 90 ft., where heath and wild flowers grow in profusion. It was once attached to the Abbey of Cerne in Dorset, and was the site of a hermit's cell. The island has a sentimental interest to all connected with the Boy Scout Movement as having been the site of the first experimental camp, organized by (then) Colonel Baden-Powell in 1907. The island is now National Trust property. About half the area is maintained as a National Reserve and on certain days guided tours are arranged. There are pleasant bathing beaches. Boats run from Poole Quay and Sandbanks at frequent intervals from April to September.

Brownsea Castle, built in the reign of Henry VIII and strengthened in Charles I's time, was an important defence to Poole, for, being at the mouth of the Harbour, it commanded all shipping passing in and out. That such control proved at times unpleasant to the shipping trade of Poole is proved by a complaint dated 1581, which placed on record that " The Goovner of Bronkseye doth molest the inhabitants of the towne, and will not suffer them to passe any persons from Northaven Point, butt doth take ther monye from them, which is not only a great hindrance to poor men that were woonte to gayne that wayse, but also an infryninge of our liberties, wherefore wee think yt verye necessarye to be remedyd." Nothing seems to have resulted from this protest, for we find that subsequently the high-handed " Goovner " added deeds to his threats and shot at the *Bountiful Gift,* killing Walter Meryatt, its owner and captain. During the Civil War the Castle was held by a Parliament garrison. Afterwards it was used simply as a dwelling-house, with additions made to it from time to time. Lieutenant-Colonel Waugh, who came into possession of Branksea Island in 1848, spent large sums in trying to develop its resources, in building cottages and a beautiful little church, and in transforming the rather bare-looking Castle into a palatial mansion with a Tudor-Gothic front. Having been burned down in 1896, it was rebuilt and the interior was remodelled.

The surroundings of this island-dotted water are full of interest. There is **Ower,** with its interesting sea-gull pond; and **Wytch,** once the flourishing port of Corfe Castle, and now, with its two houses, not uncomfortably over-populated. In one direction is **Arne,** a picturesque village with a tiny church, and not a single inn or shop; and in another **Russell Quay,** with its large heronry.

A delightful water trip is by way of that arm of the Harbour where there is a confluence of three waters—the creek of Middlebere; the Corfe River that debouches at Wytch Passage House, the ancient port of Corfe Castle; and the Upper Bushey. Motor ferries ply across various parts of the Harbour from Poole Quay and Sandbanks.

POOLE

Access.—Rail from London, the Midlands and North. Bus from Bournemouth, Swanage, etc. Nearest airport is at Christchurch, 10 miles away. Launches to Studland, Swanage and Wareham.
Early Closing.—Wednesday.
Information Bureau.—Municipal Buildings, Civic Centre, Park Gates East.

Population.—97,520.
Sport and Entertainment. — Bathing, Bowls, Golf, Putting, Cricket, Riding, Sailing, Rowing, Squash Rackets, Tennis. Speedway and Greyhound tracks, Bowling Centre. For more detailed information, see our *Guide to Bournemouth and Poole.*

Poole is a town of ancient lineage which of recent years has made wonderful progress.

The **Church,** originally a chapel-of-ease to Canford, was erected in 1820. The **Guildhall** was built in 1761. During smuggling days, Poole was the headquarters of the celebrated Harry Paye, or " Arripay," as the Spaniards who so dreaded him rendered the name. He is said to have brought into Poole Harbour, on one occasion, more than a hundred prizes, and " to have scoured the Channel of Flanders so powerfully that no ship could pass that way without being taken."

The Old Town House is a fine example of a fifteenth-century Guild Hall (*open*).

Two finds of Roman coins have recently been unearthed, each of some thousand coins. Other relics of interest are the ancient Town cellars and Jail in Thames Street, some footings of the old Town Wall and a postern gate in St. Clement's Lane. Mention must also be made of the very fine municipal buildings erected in 1932, and the new industrial research laboratories near the harbour.

Poole has in recent years made considerable strides as a holiday resort, and **Branksome, Branksome Dene, Canford Cliffs** and **Sandbanks** are already as well known as larger and older spots beyond the Borough boundary. Sandbanks is a fine centre for bathing and boating trips. In addition to the car-carrying ferry, a considerable number of smaller craft are continually crossing to and from South Haven, Sandbanks, Shell Beach, etc.; and boats also run along the coast to Studland and Swanage.

Towards the eastern end of the Quay are the works of Poole Pottery Ltd., where visitors are enabled to see the fascinating processes by which **Poole Pottery** is fashioned. Among other crafts, here may be seen " throwing " and the hand painting of giftwares for which Poole Pottery is world famous. The works are open Monday to Friday 9.30–4.00. The tour, including the services of a qualified guide, costs 1s. Visitors are advised to book in advance by telephone—Poole 2866.

Corfe

Routes *from Swanage—*
(*a*) By train. On certain days cheap tickets are issued.
(*b*) By road, six miles *via* Kingston, or 4½ *via* the Valley Road.
For particulars respecting bus services and coach excursions, *see* current announcements.

(*c*) By footpath over the Downs, about 6 miles (*see* p. 128).
Hotels.—*Bankes Arms, Greyhound.*
Model of castle, church and square in garden of large house just off the Square, 2s.

Many of Corfe's visitors come merely to see the Castle, thinking it the sole attraction, but the entire village, from the ancient ruins to the more modern War Memorial, forms such a complete and satisfying entity that one feels a whole holiday would not be too long to exhaust its charm. It is, indeed, becoming increasingly popular as a holiday resort, since, in addition to its own beauty, it is an excellent centre for exploring the country. The rare " Man Orchid " grows on the hills round Corfe.

Accommodation may be obtained at many of the cottages as well as at the picturesque inns.

Its situation is extraordinarily impressive, the Castle on its hill dominating the one gap in the solid line of the Purbecks. Perhaps the most striking views are obtained from the flat Wareham road, but it is almost as fine when seen from the ridge. It may almost be said that town and Castle are literally one, because undoubtedly, after the attempted destruction of the latter by the Parliamentarians, the people found heaven-sent material at hand and made full use of it in the stoutly built grey-walled, grey-roofed cottages that cluster round the church and Castle. They seem superior in pattern and size to the ordinary little village dwelling, and a few have, above their doorways, stones engraved in geometrical designs, which were the work of the famous Purbeck Marblers.

The apex of the tiny town, with a steep approach from the Wareham side, is the little Square, flanked on one side by the church and on the others by old inns and houses, gay with flowers, while the Castle, on its hill behind, dominates the whole. In the Square are the steps of the fourteenth-century Cross, surmounted by a shaft and cross to commemorate Queen Victoria's Diamond Jubilee.

The Town Hall in West Street is of interest in having a stone-built ground floor with a brick-built upper storey added later. On the ground floor is a museum of oddments and local tools while above is the council chamber and court room with interesting pictures and arms of the Constables of the castle.

Standing a little back from the Swanage road, which runs past the end of the church, is the small Elizabethan manor house of Dacombes, now called *Morton's House*.

Corfe Church

is dedicated to St. Edward, King and Martyr, the youthful king whose tragic fate is the subject of one of the best-known stories in school history books (*see* under Corfe Castle). It is of great interest both historically and architecturally. With the exception of the tower, which dates from the end of the fourteenth century, the church was rebuilt in 1859.

The original church was used by Parliamentary troops when the castle was besieged. Considerable restoration was carried out in 1947 under the direction of the late Martin Travers, resulting in improvement to the chancel and sanctuary. The church was a Royal Peculiar, and the Rector and Choir still wear the red cassocks.

The west doorway is in the Perpendicular style of the time of Henry VII. The north porch with pillars and capitals is a copy of the original and is worthy of a cathedral. The carving was recut at the time of the rebuilding. The pillars in the nave are Norman work and part of the original church. The Early English

141

chancel, of Purbeck stone, has windows worthy of notice by reason of the various styles they exhibit, and in the baptistery are two marble shafts originally in the earlier building, which suffered greatly during the siege of the Castle, the lead roof and organ pipes being used by the Parliamentary forces for making shot. The tower arch is an excellent example of the Perpendicular style. Among other objects of interest are the stone coffin of an infant, diminutive coffin lid of Purbeck marble for heart burial, and thirteenth-century coffin slabs, the fourteenth-century font, releaded; the church-wardens' chest in the south aisle, for the making of which one Hy. Paulett was paid in 1672 the sum of 8s.; old stones found in pulling down the church before rebuilding; and on the north wall a plan of the Chapel floor as partly relaid in 1941 with ledgers from the outside pavement and churchyard with inscriptions. Over the north door are the arms of Charles II.

The **Tower** has some quaint gargoyles. From its prospect it is easy to understand that the Roundheads found it useful as the site of a battery during the siege. There are six bells, one of which is dated 1739.

There are many quaint old records, dating from 1563, stored among the church documents. The burial registers date from 1695 and all persons are recorded to have been buried in woollen shrouds to conform to the act passed by Charles II in 1678. This was to benefit the woollen industry and was not repealed until 1810.

Facing the Square and with its back to the churchyard is a delightful old house, on the first floor of which is a large chamber with a delicate stone bow-fronted window. Originally it was the Mayor's robing room.

Corfe Castle

Admission.—1s. The Castle grounds are open from 10 a.m. till dusk.
Guide Book (authorized edition), 2s. Contains a good historical account of the Castle and its varied fortunes.

Across the Square, houses and shops stand on the edge of the outer moat which cuts off connection with the lower levels. On the other side of the outer bridge is the **Gate Tower**, flanked by two round towers, 20 ft. in diameter. In ancient days a drawbridge spanned the twenty-five feet between the bridge and the castle gate. The towers seen leaning at all angles owe their inclination to the explosive force of Parliamentary gunpowder in 1646. The gateway leads into the first ward, or tilting-court, now a green lawn. Its defences were constructed by Edward I, 1280. They comprised six towers in addition to those at the entrance and a curtain wall seven feet thick in one part, twelve in another.

The first ward slopes up to the gateway to the second where there was a drawbridge over a moat cut into the solid rock. The right-hand tower of the gateway occupies its original position. The tower on the left was displaced by the attempt to overthrow it by undermining. The extent of the displacement is shown by the relative position of the two portions of the ruptured arch. There were two portcullises, as proved by the grooves in which they worked. Between the outer portcullis and the position of the gate are the holes for the counter-weights of the portcullises.

On the left of the outer wall of the second ward is some herring-bone masonry which was the undercroft of some pre-Norman building. A short distance farther, at the extreme west of the Castle, is the tower, beneath which was a dark, damp dungeon. The buildings on the summit of the hill formed **The Keep**, the Castle proper. To ease the ascent to it the path was made to wind through the greater part of the exterior wards in succession, which were so planned that each formed a subordinate fortress.

The Castle would have remained impregnable until long after the period of its destruction by Cromwell had treachery not been at work. Against modern weapons Corfe Castle would of course not be tenable for an hour; but in earlier days, against short-range guns, the stronghold defied any attack. Even now the great walls, agape and with sightless windows, proudly tell of former strength and defiance. Excellent workmanship was displayed throughout the building. Solidity, strength and permanence were the first considerations, but the hard, grim lines of the fortress were relieved wherever possible (as in the stone mouldings of door frames and windows) with a suggestion of Classic ornament.

Historical Note

Corfe was once Corfesgeat, Hardy calling it " Corvesgate," or, in some of the earlier editions, " Coomb Castle." The word signifies a " cutting," as the position proclaims. It is derived from the A.S. *coerfan*, to cut, and is found also in Dorset at Coryates (Corfegates) and Corton (Corf-town), both near Portesham.

Stephen laid waste Wareham Castle, but he could not take Corfe. King John used the place as a royal residence, and kept his regalia here for security. He likewise imprisoned and starved to death twenty-two French nobles in the dungeons, and the castle earned for itself the ominous title of " The Royal Prison of Purbeck." In Edward I's reign the Castle was strengthened and in parts rebuilt. Successive sovereigns resided here, and Henry VIII added to the fortifications.

Queen Elizabeth sold the Castle to Sir Christopher Hatton. After his death it was bought (1635) by Attorney-General Sir John Bankes, afterwards Lord Chief Justice and it is still owned by his descendants. Lady Bankes, daughter of Nicholas Martyn, of Puddletown, in the absence of her husband, defended the fortress against various attacks by the Parliamentarians, although the garrison consisted only of a few retainers and servants, until Prince Maurice brought help. Later, Sir Walter Erle, with a strong force, vainly attempted to rush the Castle with a simultaneous attack on all sides. In 1646 Corfe was again besieged, and the attacking force, being treacherously admitted, obtained possession of the famous pile.

EXCURSIONS FROM CORFE

Gun Ranges.—A considerable portion of the country east of Lulworth, including Tyneham and Worbarrow, are used for gun practice. The area covered by the ranges is clearly defined by notice boards, signs and flags. Certain roads over the ranges are open when there is no firing but the road to Tyneham is only open to traffic when the Gunnery School is closed for the purpose of leave. The dates this road is open are published weekly in the issues of the *Bournemouth Echo* and *Dorset Daily Echo*.

I.—TO KINGSTON

By road, two miles south of Corfe. It is on the bus route between Wareham and Swanage.

(*a*) *For walking*, take one of the footpaths between the cottages on the right and bear away to the left over the fields (Corfe Common) until the road is regained.

(*b*) *For motoring*, keep to the main Swanage road for a mile and at the fork bear right and mount the hill, which is very steep. Overhanging trees afford a welcome shade in summer.

Kingston, with its remarkable memorial church, is described on p. 134.

In walking up West Street, Corfe, the church can be seen on the hills in front.

Durlston Bay (*Valentine*)

Studland Bay (*John T. Etches*)

Lulworth Cove   (*John T. Etches*)

Corfe and the Castle   (*Valentine*)

II.—TO CHURCH KNOWLE

A pretty walk of one and a half miles westward. The walk starts through the gate on to the common at the end of West Street and away to the right in the direction of the near range of hills. The path wanders beside a stream over-hung with willows, a pleasant spot for a picnic. On reaching the road turn to left. **Church Knowle** has an inn and a number of pretty, flower-covered cottages. The thirteenth-century Church stands at the east end of the village. Though so very small, it contains in the north transept a canopied altar-tomb with brasses to John Clavell, 1572. The chancel has three stone arches with two hagioscopes.

Beyond the village is a farm-house, formerly the manor house of **Barneston.** Much of the building is untouched thirteenth-century work. Barneston preserves the name of Bern, the Saxon who held the manor under the Conqueror.

III.—TO CREECH GRANGE, RETURNING *viâ* STOBOROUGH

This excursion of about ten miles includes one of the finest and most extensive panoramic views in Dorset.

To Church Knowle as above. About half a mile beyond the village turn to right. The road mounts the hill and merges into a cart-track over fields. From the highest point of 655 ft. a marvellous view is obtained—from Bournemouth and the Isle of Wight in the east to Hardy's Monument at Portesham, westward beyond Weymouth. (From Hardy's Monument to Creech Barrow is twenty-one miles in a straight line.) Weymouth and Portland are easily distinguished. **Creech Barrow Hill** is the mound a quarter mile north of the cart-track.

Continue past **Bond's Folly**—a stone façade with three windows and nothing else—well worthy of the name.

Beyond the Folly go through two gates and turn off imme-diately on the right through a white gate. A fairly good road now leads downhill past the beautiful **Creech Grange** estate. On reaching the main Wareham road at **Stoborough** turn sharply to the right. In two miles is the *Half-way Inn,* and in another two miles Corfe is regained.

IV.—TO KIMMERIDGE

Five miles by road from Corfe.

To Church Knowle as in Route II, bearing to left at sign-post, in the direction of Puddlemill and Bradle if on foot. The continuing road marked Kimmeridge is the larger main route for cars. At Bradle Farm turn left up hill, then follow the line of telegraph poles to Smedmore Hill. The village of **Kimmeridge** is gained in another mile and a half. It stands a mile inland at a height of over 300 ft. and consists mainly of a few thatched cottages. It has a small plain stone church (St. Nicholas) in the Norman and Decorated styles, with an ancient font, and turret for one bell. **Kimmeridge Bay,** or Cove, in many respects resembles Chapman's Pool in appearance (p. 132), and also was connected with smuggling.

There is a good motor road through the Smedmore estate to the sea. *Toll. Beach car parking, free.*

Two miles to the west is **Worbarrow Bay** (p. 150), with its fine cliff formation of great interest to geologists. Here can be seen in contrasting colours the outcrop of the different Purbeck strata.

V.—TO EAST LULWORTH

About nine miles, *via* Church Knowle and the right-hand fork past Steeple (church has Norman work) and so on to the ridge of the Purbecks. This road is open only at certain times. The village and Castle are described on pp. 148–50.

VI.—THE BLUE POOL

The **Blue Pool** is the largest of many small lakes scattered over Wareham Heath which occupy the site of old clay pits. Its colour is due to finely suspended clay particles. It is reached from the Corfe to Wareham road by a turning to the left one and a quarter miles short of the latter town. A drive through attractive woods leads to a gate where tickets may be obtained. (*Admission fee, car park.*) The Pool lies in a beautiful setting of trees and sandhills, the green and yellow making a brilliant foil for the deep blue of the water. Bathing is prohibited.

Wool, Bindon Abbey, Lulworth, Bovington and Moreton

Access.—*Rail.*—Wool Station is on the Southern Region line, six miles west of Wareham.
    Road.—By car, bus and coach along excellent roads from Weymouth, Wareham, Swanage and Lulworth.
    Wool is on the main Wareham-Dorchester road, about 3 miles west of Wareham.

The red-brick Jacobean **Wool Manor House,** now a farm, which was once the residence of the D'Urberville (or Turberville) family, can be seen well from the train, when coming from Wareham, and it is only five minutes' walk from the up-side of the station. Readers of Hardy's *Tess* will remember the pathetic incidents of the honeymoon at Wellbridge (Wool Bridge) House. The house is named from the quaint Elizabethan **Bridge** that here spans the reed-fringed river *Frome.* The bridge is composed of five semicircular arches supported by strong ribs placed beneath. Each arcade is divided by a triangular buttress, which, at the road level, forms a recess for foot passengers.

About twice as far from the station, on the opposite side of the line, is—

Bindon Abbey

(Admission, *daily*, charge.)

From the station approach turn left and shortly, where the road divides, go to the left again. At the next fork go to the right and in a few yards the entrance gate will be seen on the left, about half a mile from the station.
Permission must be obtained by those wishing to sketch or take photographs. The grounds are closed at 7 p.m. in summer, dusk in winter.

Entering by the pretty castellated red-brick **Gatehouse,** visitors are free to wander through the grounds away from the house. The Abbey was founded in 1172 by Robert de Newburgh, for Cistercian monks, but ruthless destruction has left only the foundations, with ivy-clad walls a few feet high. Near the site of the high altar is a stone coffin mentioned in Thomas Hardy's novel "Tess of the D'Urbervilles." The coffin is 7 feet long and is possibly associated with a massive grave slab of an abbot. The brass has vanished, but around the matrix or casement of the slab is an inscription in Lombardic capitals to "ABBAS RICARDVS DE MANERS." Many pieces of carved stone may also be seen including a sepulchral statue of a child known as the "Boy Bishop." The precincts, includng the ruins and fishponds cover some ten acres. Large portions of the structure were standing as late as 1733, when they were drawn and engraved by Buck.

The Abbey is owned by the Weld family, of whom more below. It was at Bindon Mills that Angel Clare worked.

About two miles west of Wool is Winfrith Heath where are the laboratories of part of the Reactor Group of the Atomic Energy Authority. At present the site can be viewed from almost any direction, but a screen of trees will eventually hide it.

Wool to Lulworth.—The five-mile ride southward from Wool station over the hilly country-side is of great interest. The road at one part rises to a height of nearly 500 ft., and there is a glorious view backward over a great part of Dorset. Lulworth Castle lies in the trees on the left as the Cove is approached. The road from East Lulworth now joins, and there is a steep winding descent through a gap in the hills to the tiny inlet. The villages, both of East and West Lulworth, are rather shadowed by the popular appeal of the Cove, but they have picturesque thatched cottages and handsome churches.

LULWORTH COVE

Access.—Lulworth Cove is reached from Swanage or Weymouth by train, coach, bus or car. From Swanage it is 17½ miles distant.

(a) *By Rail.*—The nearest station is *Wool (Southern Region).*

From *Swanage* the route is by rail to Wareham, changing for Wool.

Buses run between station and Cove several times daily.

(b) *By Road.*—Coaches run from Swanage (17½ miles), by the high road which passes through Corfe, Holme Lane (one of the prettiest lanes in the country), East Lulworth and Lulworth West, half a mile short of the Cove.

Bathing.—Convenient; pebbly cove, but several sandy bathing beaches.

Boating.—Rowing boats for hire.

Car Parks.—There is a well-regulated park at the entrance to the Cove. There is another adjoining the Restaurant opposite the *Cove Hotel.*

Teas, etc., at the large Restaurant by the upper Car Park, at the hotel and at several tea-rooms. Lobster teas are very popular.

Lulworth Cove, a little oyster-shaped inlet, is perhaps the most beautiful bit of the Dorset coast, lying almost hidden by frowning cliffs whose contorted strata bear witness to rock-folding on a grand scale in the far-distant past. The blue sky, tilted grey cliffs crowned with emerald turf and trees of darker shade embowering little stone cottages, make one of those static pictures that remain clear, printed into the mind long after others have become blurred into general impressions.

Over seven thousand acres to the north and east of Lulworth Cove are in the possession of the Ministry of Defence (Army Department) and are used extensively for firing exercises by the R.A.C. Gunnery School, Lulworth Camp. The roads leading to East and West Lulworth are closed during firing but reopened to the public when firing ceases. However, the road joining East and West Lulworth is always open. The footpaths are closed. The road through Tyneham Valley to Worbarrow Bay is open during public holidays and the month of August.

Visitors whose time is limited should at once ascend the cliff on the *western side*. Then either turn seaward for the fine view from the headland, or rightward for the cliff path leading westward. This is the direction for the best view of the Cove, and worth travelling miles to see.

The pleasantest way to see the cliffs and coves is to take a boat. Rounding **Nelson Fort,** several fine caves are reached at **Stair Hole,** Their structure is unique. In one, great pillars of rock rise from the water and support the gigantic superstructure, quite meriting the name **Cathedral Cavern.** A fine bay, with sandy beach, follows, then come the charming **St. Oswald Bay** and **Man o' War Bay,** where the bathing is excellent. Beyond, at about a mile from the Cove, is the **Durdle Door,** a large natural arch some 40 ft. high and wide.

To reach the Durdle Door by the cliffs is not more than an hour's walk. Go through the car park, up the well-defined white track up the hill, and follow the cliff path until the Door is reached. A mile farther, where a perpendicular white cliff rises from the beach, there is another arch tunnelled out by the waves. Provision has been made for camping near Durdle Door on reserved ground, with water supply, modern sanitation and general store. At low tide it is possible to return to Lulworth Cove by way of the sands *viâ* **Man o' War Bay** and **St. Oswald's Bay.**

Sloping to the sea on the *east* side of the Cove is a wonderful **Fossil Forest.** Among the marvels are fossilized stumps of trees. with the whole inside gone, standing as they have stood for ages. They are large enough to hold several people.

Almost overlooking the Cove are the remains of **Little Bindon Abbey,** associated with the great Cistercian house near Wool.

Two miles east of the Cove is **Worbarrow Bay,** where the stratified cliff scenery is considered by many even finer than that displayed at Lulworth Cove.

Lulworth Castle,

at East Lulworth, stands in a beautiful park about two miles from the Cove. Built at the end of the sixteenth century, it was considered one of the most perfect Jacobean mansions in the country,

but it was partly destroyed by fire in August, 1929. The walls of the Castle remain very little changed, but danger notices warn the public not to approach them closely for fear of falling masonry.

There is free admittance through the Park on Sundays for service at both the Catholic Church and East Lulworth Parish Church which stand in the grounds.

The stables have recently been converted to house the family art collection removed here from Ince Blundell Hall, Lancashire. For availability for view see local announcements.

The Castle was erected in 1588, and for generations has belonged to the Welds, a Roman Catholic family of whom the famous Cardinal Weld was a prominent member. Another member of the family may be regarded as the founder in this country of Stonyhurst, the great Roman Catholic School. The seminary was originally founded abroad in 1592 to provide an education for English Catholics whose schooling at home was rendered impossible by the penal laws, but it was Mr. Weld of Lulworth who first offered it an asylum at his hall of Stonyhurst, where the College was re-opened in 1794.

Thomas Weld enjoyed the friendship of George III, who often paid visits to Lulworth when residing at Weymouth. An ardent Catholic, he asked leave of the King to build a chapel. The King gave his permission on condition that it was built in the form of a temple. This chapel stands in the park, and was the first Roman Catholic Church built openly in England after the Reformation. Though of curious shape its interior decoration is beautiful and striking. Below it is the crypt of the Weld family. Thomas Weld was also instrumental in bringing to this country the community of which his daughter was a member in order to escape from the Revolution in France.

The Welds of Lulworth are entitled to present a silver basin with water for the King's hands at the Coronation. The claim comes to them through the ownership of the adjacent manor of Winfrith.

Away to the right are the cove and cliffs of **Arish Mel Gap**, with its monastery farm, founded in 1794 by Thomas Weld, sen., and his son Thomas, for Trappist monks.

Bovington and Moreton

A large area of the heathland to the north-west of Wool is occupied by Bovington Camp, almost a town in itself, and easily reached from Wareham, Wool or Dorchester. Of great interest is the Royal Armoured Corps *Tank Museum* (open weekdays 10–12.30 and 2–4.45; and Saturdays, Sundays and Bank Holidays, 10.30–12.30 and 2–4. Free.)

The Museum comprises a unique collection of tanks and armoured cars which is unequalled anywhere else in the world. Tanks of other nations are included but the bulk of the collection consists of British and American tanks and armoured cars. There is also a large number of interesting exhibits connected with tanks and armoured warfare generally.

Clouds Hill Cottage

A little over a mile north of Bovington Camp, on the Bere Regis road, is Clouds Hill Cottage where Col. T. E. Lawrence (Lawrence of Arabia) lived during the latter years of his stirring and adventurous life. Over the door the words " Nothing Matters " are inscribed in Greek. The cottage, presented to the National Trust in 1937, is open on Sundays, Wednesdays and Thursdays, 2–6 p.m. (April–September), and noon to dusk (October–March), admission charge.

Lawrence of Arabia served for two years in the Tank Corps and whilst at Bovington Camp rented the small cottage at Clouds Hill. In 1925 he rejoined the Royal Air Force and served as an aircraftman for ten years, during which time he purchased the cottage. All too soon after his retirement he was killed in a fall from his motor-cycle on the road near by. He was buried in the cemetery at Moreton village. The grave has a plain stone slab with carved top touchingly inscribed, " To the Dear memory of T. E. Lawrence, Fellow of All Souls' College, Oxford," and " Dominus Illuminatio Mea " (The Lord is my Light).

After Lawrence's death, Eric Kennington carved a memorial in the form of a recumbent effigy in Arab dress, and which can be found in St. Martin's Church, Wareham (*see* p. 153).

Moreton Church has been rebuilt several times. Its engraved glass apse windows by Laurence Whistler are of considerable note.

Wareham

Access.—Wareham, 120¼ miles from London, is on the Southern Region main line to Dorchester and Weymouth, and is the junction of the Isle of Purbeck line to Corfe and Swanage.

It comes as a surprise to many strangers to find that the town, in addition to its rail connections with Bournemouth and Swanage, can also be reached by water from Poole Harbour.

Buses and coaches connect Wareham with Swanage, Weymouth, Lulworth Cove and Bournemouth, and, in the season, centres in the Midlands and West as well as London. Wareham is at the junction of the excellent roads from Weymouth and Swanage to Poole.

Cinema.—*Rex Theatre*, West Street.

Early Closing Day.—Wednesday.

Fishing.—Good coarse fishing. Free water at Wareham Pool and at the Swanage railway bridge (from a boat). Licences necessary from the Avon and Dorset River Authority.

Golf.—There is a nine-hole golf course on the Poole road, about 6 minutes from the station.

Hotels.—*Red Lion, Black Bear, Antelope.*

Market Day.—Thursday.

Population.—3,490.

River Trips.—There are plenty of boats for hire; by motor-boat pleasant trips can be had along the river Frome to Poole Harbour.

Tennis.—Hard court in Recreation Ground.

Wareham is an interesting as well as a beautiful town, with many indications of former importance in the broad layout of its streets, its fine churches and picturesque old inns. Although it is a somewhat quiet drowsy little place with old-fashioned shops and many pleasant houses of warm red brick and a weekly market, its main streets are filled with a never-ending stream of cars and coaches. The old market place, opposite the *Horse and Groom*, is now used as a car park while another exists at the old Quay by the riverside. The two other big hostelries are the *Black Bear* and *Red Lion*, both excellent examples of a real old-fashioned English inn. Wareham, near heathland, sea, river and harbour, is an excellent holiday centre.

The discovery of Roman coins and pottery, the direction of the principal streets, and traces of a Roman road from Wareham to Dorchester point to the site of the town having been occupied by the Romans, but the barrows on the heath point to still earlier occupation.

Wareham was the burial place of Brictric, king of the West Saxons, under the Heptarchy, in A.D. 800, and during the Danish invasions war raged for a century and a half.

In 876 the Wareham stronghold and the Nunnery were destroyed by the Danes. The body of the young Saxon King, Edward the Martyr, murdered at Corfe, was buried in Wareham Church. In 1015 Canute ravaged the neighbourhood. In 1138, Robert de Lincoln seized the town and castle for the Empress Maud. The town supplied Edward III with three ships and fifty-nine men for the siege of Calais. The manor of Wareham, both before and after the Conquest, was part of the demesnes of the Crown, and in the reign of Henry VIII the lordship and manor was granted successively to the Queens, Jane Seymour, Catherine Howard, and Catherine Parr. In 1610 the manorial rights were sold to the then mayor, Thomas Haynes, and others.

There was a disastrous fire in 1762, for which the Sun Fire Office paid considerable sums in compensation. The town was later rebuilt under strict conditions forbidding the use of thatch. A charter was granted by Queen Anne in 1703.

Entering the town by road from Swanage, the parish church will be seen on the right. Coming by roads which cross the railway near the station, the town is entered at its opposite (the northern) end, against the ancient Church of St. Martin. Coming from Weymouth, the parish church will be to the right and St. Martin's to the left.

From the Station to the bridge over the river *Puddle* (*Piddle* or *Trent*) at the entrance to the town, is a walk of five minutes. Just after crossing the bridge notice the *Lord Nelson Inn*. It is a useful landmark, as here, both right and left of the main road, are approaches to the old earthen walls. A few yards farther there is, on the left, perched above the road—

St. Martin's Church

This old Church, only 45 feet long, is visited by antiquaries from all parts of the country. It is said to have owed its origin to St. Aldhelm, the first bishop of Sherborne, in 705, and it is the traditional burial-place of Brictric.

In 1762 many homeless families found shelter, during the great fire of Wareham, in St. Martin's Church, which had been disused since 1736, but from then until the end of 1936 the old church had only been used for a commemorative service in connection with Queen Victoria's Jubilee in 1887 and some christenings in the same year. In 1935 the Archdeacon of Dorset formed a committee to save it from further decay and furnish it for Divine Worship. The restoration is simple and very beautiful, and is recorded by a tablet in the porch with the following inscription: " After two centuries of silent witness this ancient church of St. Martin was rededicated to the service of Almighty God by Neville, Lord Bishop of Salis-

bury, 23rd November, 1936." Services are now held in it on weekdays. In 1939 the effigy of T. E. Lawrence was presented by his

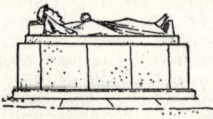

brother. It is the work of Mr. Eric Kennington, and represents Lawrence lying at
full length in Arab dress, his right hand
grasping the hilt of a curved dagger, with
his whip by his side. His head lies on a
camel's saddle, beside which is a pile of his
three favourite books.

Lawrence frequently visited Wareham during the last years of
his life.

The church to-day still shows traces of Anglo-Saxon masonry. It was
probably rebuilt about 1020 and added to in early Norman times, while
additions and alterations were made during the next three or four
hundred years. The low chancel arch, with two hagioscopes at the side,
is early Norman, and the North Arcade pointed arches, and pillars with
Purbeck marble caps, are thirteenth century. The windows are rather
later, while the font and bell are of seventeenth-century date.

By the altar is a door which may be a relic of the Christian super-
stition that the Devil fled through it when the bells began to ring.

There are many traces of colour decoration of early date on the walls,
fragments of Elizabethan black-letter texts, and an eighteenth-century
memorial inscription to Carruthers and his wife, who died of "typhus
favour."

During the recent renovation more wall paintings were uncovered and
in 1940 a remarkable variety of fragments of wall decorations ranging
from the twelfth to the eighteenth century were exposed. In 1942 the
church was damaged by bombs, which completely destroyed the neighbouring houses.

At the Town Hall in North Street, there is a right-angled
turn to the left, East Street. On the right-hand side are
Streche's Almshouses, endowed in 1418 for " six antient men
and five women " as the inscription (a relic of the former
building) quaintly records. They are now let out as private and
business premises, as modern almshouses have been erected
at Westport. At the lower end of East Street the weekly cattle
market is held on Thursdays, when farmers for miles around
attend, and there is a comforting display of cattle, pigs and
poultry, especially pigs. Returning to the main street, and
continuing nearly to the bridge, a turn to the left leads to the
old Market Square, now a car park. On the farther side a
turning to right leads to—

The Church of Lady St. Mary

Heterogeneous in style owing to restorations which replaced the Saxon nave by the existing one built in 1841, the church still contains many features and objects of interest.

The unique lead font of the twelfth century rests upon a base of Purbeck marble of a century later. In high relief around the bowl are the figures of the twelve apostles much disfigured. It is said that the damage was done by Cromwell's soldiers. Near the font, at the west end of the north aisle, is a vestry, originally one of four side chapels.

On the floor at the east end of the north aisle are some ancient stones. Let into the wall is a stone carving of Christ on the Cross with the Virgin on one side and St. John on the other. This was formerly on the outside of a porch. Just below is part of an inscription about 1,300 years old. It is believed to refer to a famous British missionary, whose name is found in ancient Welsh writings. Among the stones on the floor is a cresset, or lamp, with five bowls, in each of which a wick floated in oil, and stones recording the names of two of the Danish chiefs who drove Alfred out of Wareham. There are the remains of two stone altars upon which the Roman settlement are said to have worshipped their gods by burning incense; since there is nothing to identify them in this connection it is more likely that they are parts of an early Saxon building. The double piscina in the wall came from one of the side chapels and dates back to about 1280. One basin was used for the ceremonial washing of hands and the other for the washing of the sacred vessels.

At the east end of the south aisle are steps leading down to the beautifully restored Chapel of King Edward the Martyr. The chapel was here for centuries before the large church was built round it. The body of the boy king murdered at Corfe Castle in 978 was buried in this chapel. Two years later the monks of Shaftesbury removed the body to their monastery, leaving the heavy coffin behind.

Above King Edward's chapel is another chapel. Its history is not known. The doorway, of Norman work, is behind the choir stalls. On the south of the Sanctuary, which was restored in 1937, is the Becket Chapel built in the hollow of a great stone buttress. "The plate of the Holy Loaf," in blue and white pottery, hangs above the double piscina.

The two immense Purbeck effigies in the chancel are among the first specimens of their kind in Dorset and are said to be of Henry d'Estoke (*circa* 1240) and Sir William d'Estoke (d. 1294).

On the south side of St. Mary's Church is **Wareham Priory,** founded by St. Aldhelm and therefore one of the most

ancient in the country. It was shorn of its ecclesiastical glory in the reign of Henry VIII, and the building remaining is used as a private house, said to be the oldest occupied dwelling in Dorset. With its old red tiles and riverside lawn it makes a charming picture.

Motor traffic led to the demolition in 1925 of the old bridge of five arches which here crossed the Frome and to its replacement by a wider bridge of three arches.

The road leads to Corfe, 4½ miles, and Swanage.

Re-entering the town, **Holy Trinity Church,** now disused, is almost at once passed on the left. Beyond it the lane on the left passes the Rectory, a lovely old house and garden surrounded by an ancient stone wall showing a blocked-up Norman archway with herring-bone carving. John Hutchins, the author of the well-known book *History and Antiquities of Dorset,* lived here as parish priest from 1743 to 1773. At the end of the lane are—

The Town Walls,

grassy ramparts which are leased by the Town Council as open spaces. Seats are provided, which command fine views over the surrounding country.

Of the origin of these earthworks nothing can be said with certainty. They may have been constructed by the Romans, or possibly by the Britons. They were formerly much higher, and were finally dismantled in the Civil War. They stand on the north, east and west sides of the town, the south being protected by the Frome. The defence was strengthened by a ditch outside the walls and connecting the Frome and the Piddle. The highest part of the west wall is known as *Bloody Bank,* from having been the scene of the execution, by order of Judge Jeffreys, of some of Monmouth's unfortunate adherents. A little farther is the north-west angle. It encloses a semicircular hollow which may have been the Roman amphitheatre. A little farther on there is a bridge over the Piddle or Trent at the site of the Old Mill. The lofty chimney, which is such a prominent object in the view, is at a pottery, established for the manufacture of Staffordshire Ware.

Wareham Clay has been used for many purposes besides pottery. There was once a considerable export of tobacco-pipe clay, though no local manufacture because of the absence of suitable sand and fuel. At the present day clay for medicinal purposes is exported.

On the other side of the main road a lane by the side of the *Lord Nelson Inn* leads to another portion of the walls. At the end of the final section a lane on the right goes towards St. Mary's Church.

Before the silting up of Poole Harbour, the sea is thought to have come right up to Wareham's ramparts, and in the period when the Danes were troublesome, the mouth of the Frome was only about a mile east of the town.

From Wareham it is a pleasant excursion across the heathlands, with an excellent motor road, to—

Bere Regis,

a pretty Dorset village some six and a half miles to the north-west.

It is a place of some historical interest and at one time had two market days weekly. The Parish Church is the main building of interest and is the burial place of the Turberville family from whom Thomas Hardy based his *Tess of the D'Urbervilles,* wherein he names Bere Regis as Kingsbere-sub-Greenhill.

The Church is of Saxon foundation and incorporates many features of interest, notably the world-famous coloured and carved roof which was given by Cardinal Morton, who was born in the parish and who died as Archbishop of Canterbury in 1500. The *tower* dates fom the reign of Henry VII and the font has been in constant use since 1140.

The church is considered one of the most charming in the county and is visited by many people daily.

Beneath the south aisle is the vault of the Turbervilles, bearing a Latin inscription signifying " The door of the Sepulchre of the ancient family of the Turbervilles, 1710." The family has completely died out in the district. Other objects of interest are an ancient altar slab, beautifully carved seat-ends, grappling hooks used to tear the thatch from a burning cottage, quaint gargoyles and amusing carvings on the Norman pillars on the south side.

The old manor house of the Turbervilles has vanished, with the exception of a wing remaining in *Court Farm.*

From Bere, Tolpuddle, described elsewhere, Milborne and some of the numerous Winterbornes can be visited.

Wareham to Poole

The drive from Wareham to Poole is of extreme interest, and seems to give an epitome of the town's history and industry. The road leaves Wareham by the level crossing at the station, fine views of the heath being obtained. Several potteries, both for machine-made and hand-made work, and the golf links are passed. Then on the right a high iron fence bounds what was once the Naval Cordite Factory, but which is now being utilized for the newer industries such as plastics. Four miles out of Wareham the inn of *St. Peter's Finger* (probably a corrupt form of St. Peter ad Vincula) stands at a junction of roads, and from Lytchett Minster onwards the way becomes increasingly urbanized.

For **Poole** and its expansive Harbour, *see* pp. 136-137.

Wareham to the Arne Promontory

A turning to the left at Stoborough on the Corfe road leads over wild and lonely heath-land to **Arne**. Cars cannot be taken right down to the shore, but must be left in the tiny village. Walkers have the advantage of an infinite number of by-ways and no park-ing difficulties, but, whether walking or driving, the views, especially over the Harbour at sunset, are varied and magnificent. The little church of St. Nicholas at Arne, attached as a Chapel of Ease to Wareham Parish, dates from the thirteenth century, and possesses a Pre-Reformation altar stone which was found buried outside the north wall of the church and restored to its place during the seven-teenth century. The east window is notable in that it is cut from one piece of stone; it gives a magnificent view over Poole harbour. Above the south door are to be seen the remains of some medieval mural paintings.

Index

Where more than one reference is given the first is usually the principal.

ABBOTSBURY, 71, 44
Agglestone, the, 128
Allington Hill, 37
Anvil Point, 124
Arish Mell Gap, 151
Arne, 138
Ashe House, 20
Askerswell, 40
Axminster, 20

BALLARD DOWN, 125
Ballard Point, 125
Barneston, 145
Beaminster, 41
Bell, Dr. Andrew, 118
Bere Regis, 157, 83
Bexington-on-Sea, 44, 77
Bincleaves, 60
Bincombe, 69
Bindon Abbey, 147, 82
Blackmoor Vale, 80
Black Ven, 25
Blagdon Hill, 75, 71
Blue Pool, the, 146
Bockhampton, 105
Bond's Folly, 145
Bothenhampton, 44
Bournemouth, 135
Bovington, 151
Bowleaze Cove, 67
Bradpole, 39
Branksome, 139
Brenscombe Hill, 129
Bride Valley, 77
Bridport, 29-35, 77
Broadmayne, 70
Broadwey, 64
Broadwindsor, 43
Brownsea Island, 137
Buckland Ripers, 67
Burton Bradstock, 44, 78
Burton Freshwater, 44, 78
Burton Cliff, 44

CAME PARK, 70
Canford Cliffs, 139
Castle Cove, 60
Cerne Abbas, 80
Cerne Abbey, 81
Cerne Giant, 82
Chalbury Camp, 82
Challow Hill, 129
Chapman's Pool, 134
Charminster, 80
Charmouth, 23

Chesil, 88
Chesil Beach, 62, 44
Chickerell, 66
Chideock, 36
Chilcombe, 44
Church Knowle, 145
Church Ope Cove, 90
Cloud's Hill, 151
Colmer's Hill, 37
Combpyne, 19
Coney's Castle, 22
Conygar Hill, 22
Corfe, 140-4
   Routes to, 128
Creech Barrow Hill, 145
Creech Grange, 145
Culliford Tree, 69

DANCING LEDGE, 124, 130
Deadman's Bay, 61
Dorchester, 93-101
Durdle Door, 149
Durlston Head, 121-3

EAST LULWORTH, 146
Easton, 91
Eggardon, 40, 104
Encombe House, 134
Eype, 36

FLEET ESTUARY, 61
Fordington St. George, 103
Forde Abbey, 26
Foreland, The, 125
Fortuneswell, 89
Fossil Forest, 149

GLOBE, THE GREAT, 123
Godlingston Farm, 128
Godmanstone, 80
Golden Cap, 25, 24

HALLELUJAH BAY, 88
Handfast Point, 125
Hardy Country, 83, 104-5
Hardy Monument, 76
Hell Stone, 76
Herringstone Manor, 70
Herston, 129
Hunters' Lodge, 22

KIMMERIDGE, 146
Kingston, 134, 130, 144

LAMBERT'S CASTLE, 22
Landslip, The, 18
Langton Herring, 66
Langton Matravers, 130
Lee Lane, 31, 77
Lewisden Hill, 43
Little Bindon Abbey, 150
Loders, 39
Lulworth, 148, 146, 83
Lyme Regis, 7-17
   Buddle Bridge, 11
   Cobb, 9
   History, 13
   Langmoor Gardens, 12
   Monmouth's Beach, 10
   Museum, 11
   Parish Church, 10
   Park Memorial Chapel, 12

MAIDEN CASTLE, 102-3, 66
Man o' War Bay, 149
Mapperton, 42
Maumbury Ring, 100
Melcombe Regis, 48
Melplash, 41
Milton Abbas, 78
Milton Abbey, 79
Moreton, 151
Musbury, 22

NAPIER'S ALMSHOUSES, 99
Nelson Fort, 149
Netherbury, 40
Nether Cerne, 80
New Forest, 136
Newton Manor, 129
Newton's Cove, 60
Nine Barrow Down, 128
Nottington, 64

OLD HARRY ROCKS, 125, 136
Old Sarum, 136
Osmington, 68
Osmington Mills, 68
Ower, 138
Owermoigne, 83

PARNHAM HOUSE, 42
Peveril Point, 120
Pilsdon, 43
Poole, 139
Portesham, 75, 71

INDEX

Portland, 85-92
  Castle, 88
  Harbour, 59, 87
  Rufus Castle, 91
Portland Bill, 92
Poundbury, 100
Poxwell, 82
Preston, 67, 69
Puckstone, The, 128
Puddletown, 105
Puddletown Heath, 105
Pulpit Rock, 92
Puncknowle, 44, 77
Purbeck Quarries, 131

RACEDOWN LODGE, 43
Radipole, 63
"Rest and be Thankful," 126
Ridge Hill, 76
Ringstead Bay, 68
Rodden, 67
Rodwell, 49, 61
Round Down, 129
Rousdon, 20
Rufus Castle, 91
Russell Quay, 138

ST. ALDHELM'S HEAD, 133, 132, 131
St. Catherine's Chapel, 79
St. Oswald Bay, 149
Salisbury, 136
Sandbanks, 137, 139
  Ferry, 138

Sandsfoot Castle, 60
Seatown, 36, 25
Scowles, 134
Shaftesbury, 84
Shell Bay, 128
Sherborne, 106
Southwell, 91
Stair Hole, 149
Stinsford, 105
Stoborough, 145
Stoke Abbot, 42
Studland, 126
Sutton Poyntz, 67, 68, 69
Swannery, 73
Swanage, 113-119
  Lock-up, Old, 116
  Mill Pond, 117
  Pier, 115
  St. Mary's Church, 117
  Town Hall, 116
  Ulwell Road, 115
Swannery, 73
Swyre, 77, 44
Swyre Head, 134
Symondsbury, 37

TILLY WHIM CAVES, 123
Tolpuddle, 97
Trent, 111

UPLODERS, 39
Uplyme, 19
Upwey, 65, 69

WAKEHAM, 91

Wareham, 152
Warmwell House, 82
Westham, 66
West Bay, 35
West Stafford, 105
Weymouth, 45-58
  Greenhill Gardens, 51
  Guildhall, 51
  Harbours, 52
  Holy Trinity Church, 51
  Melcombe Regis Gardens, 51
  Nothe, 59
  Pier, 52
  Radipole Lake and Park, 49, 54
  St. Mary's Church, 51
Whitcombe, 70
Whitcombe Canonicorum, 38
White Horse, The, 68, 82
White Nothe, 68
Whitecliff Farm, 125
Wimborne, 83
Winfrith Newburgh, 83
Winterborne Faringdon, 70
Wolfeton House, 80
Wool, 147
Worbarrow Bay, 146, 150
Worth Matravers, 130
Wyke Regis, 61-2
Wytch, 138

YOUR HELP IS REQUESTED

A great part of the success of this series is due, as we gratefully acknowledge, to the enthusiastic co-operation of readers. Changes take place, both in town and country, with such rapidity that it is difficult, even for the most alert and painstaking staff, to keep pace with them all, and the correspondents who so kindly take the trouble to inform us of alterations that come under their notice in using the books render a real service not only to us but to their fellow-readers. We confidently appeal for further help of this kind.

THE EDITOR

WARD, LOCK LIMITED,
  116, Baker Street,
    London, W.1.